MR. BRANDON'S SCHOOL BUS

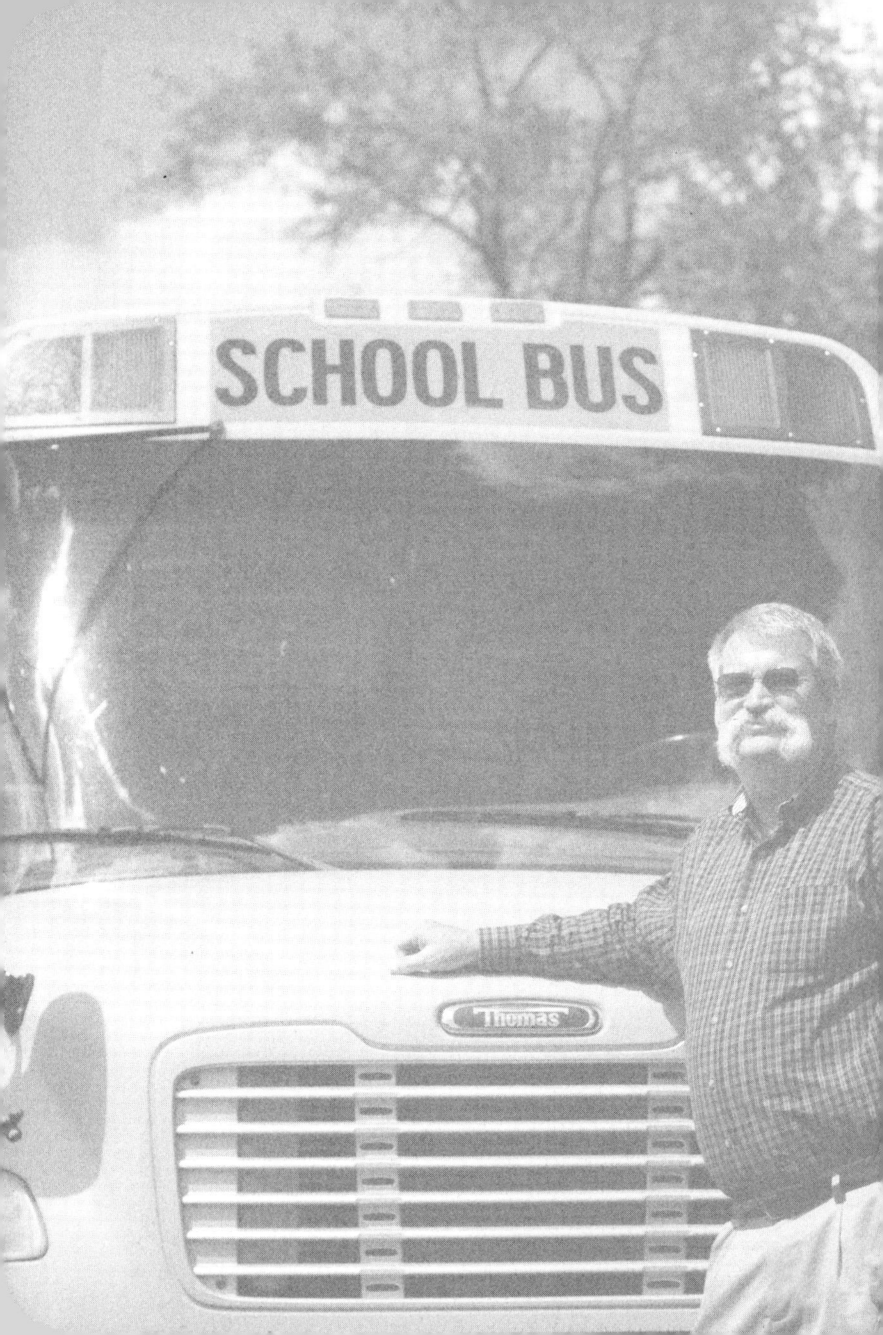
SCHOOL BUS
Thomas

Mr. Brandon's
School Bus

What I Heard
on the Way to School

TOM BRANDON

NewSouth Books

Montgomery

NewSouth Books
105 S. Court Street
Montgomery, AL 36104

Publisher's Cataloging-in-Publication data

Brandon, Tom.
Mr. Brandon's school bus : what I heard on the way to
school / Tom Brandon ; with a foreword by Larry Lee.
p. cm.

ISBN 978-1-58838-322-8 (paperback)
ISBN 978-1-60306-412-5 (ebook)

1. Bus drivers—United States—Biography. 2. School buses—
Nonfiction. 3. Education—United States. I. Title.

2016960050

Design by Randall Williams

Printed in the United States of America
by Edwards Brothers Malloy

To the greatest blessing in my life, my wife Corrine, who has patiently listened to my stories over the years and envisioned this book while I thought I was just telling funny stories to the family at supper.

Contents

Foreword

FOR THOSE OF US who call the South home, school buses are as common as Coca-Cola and kudzu. We see them throughout the school year and rarely consider that each is its own little magic kingdom where fantasies come alive and the sweet innocence of childhood sometimes meets reality.

Overseeing it all is *the* bus driver—the person entrusted with the safety of his or her young charges and the supreme being in all the realm.

Bus drivers have front-row seats for this wonderment. They make friends, stop fights, wipe tears, and offer smiles and encouragement. And they are reminded daily that childhood is a special place and time.

Tom Brandon has lived in this world for years. Twice a day he guides his big yellow bus along the back roads of rural Madison County, Alabama, hauling his cargo from home to Walnut Grove Elementary and home again. And with the keen eye and ear of a good storyteller, he has chronicled the great adventures of his riders with a talent that makes you see the smiles and hear the giggles.

I've turned to his blog time after time, always knowing a chuckle was just around the corner as he reminds us that education also happens outside the classroom.

Now he gives us a peek at his world of laughter and hurt feelings and precious innocence. Thanks to him for doing so. More importantly, thanks to him for touching so many lives.

LARRY LEE *is Alabama's foremost education blogger. Read his commentary at www.larryeducation.com. An authority on rural development, Lee is a graduate of Auburn University. He is the author of* In the Land of Cotton: How Old Times There Still Shape Alabama's Future (NewSouth, 2015); Beyond the Interstate: The Crisis in Rural Alabama; Crossroads and Connections: Strategies for Rural Alabama; *and* Lessons Learned from Rural Schools.

Preface

Tom Brandon

FOR OVER THIRTY YEARS, I have had the privilege to be a part of education. During that time, I have taught, coached, and driven the bus. Most of these years have been at a small rural school—the chickens free-ranging the school grounds are an indication of just how rural.

The school is in north Alabama and is called Walnut Grove. The members of the community know hard work and the importance of family. They talk of work, school, church, hunting, and fishing. Camouflage is considered proper attire, for men or women, for any occasion.

When established in 1920, Walnut Grove went all the way through high school; it is now a K-6 school with about 250 students.

Walnut Grove's commitment to excellence in education has won it awards on local, state, and national levels, including recognition as a National Blue Ribbon School by the U.S. Department of Education. What makes the school great is its faculty and staff and the community members who take pride in it.

Every school is unique, and Walnut Grove is no exception. We often use the phrase "Only at the Grove" to refer to the many unusual things that have happened at our little school over the years.

We celebrated Sweet Potato Day, by accident, when a farmer came unannounced to the school with an overabundant amount of sweet potatoes. We sent a bag of sweet potatoes home with each child.

One year, many months of work had been expended on a new baseball field. Opening day was looked forward to with great anticipation. But on that momentous morning, the game had to be moved to the visitors' field, for during the night there had been a light rain. The rain itself was not enough to cancel the game, but it did soften the ground. Meanwhile, the dairy cattle on the other side of the fence developed a hunger for the delicious-looking grass on the new ball field. They came through the fence and left hundreds of six-inch-deep cow tracks all over the field.

We have paraded in costume, trick-or-treated in the hallways, and held a haunted house in the locker room of the gym. Because of the school's small enrollment, we have been able to bus Walnut Grove's whole student body over to the local high school for the homecoming parade.

We have played donkey basketball. Yes, that's basketball while riding on donkeys. We've raised money in good Southern tradition by cooking chicken stew outside in big cast iron pots, held turkey shoots before Thanksgiving, and chili and bingo nights that get rather competitive. We even have a ghost.

Walnut Grove is a special place with special people. The stories that I share in this book are from my bus riders. I sincerely thank the students who have made my life richer by letting me be a part of their lives, as well as those that have ridden many miles on "Mr. Brandon's School Bus" through social media. All have encouraged me to put these stories into print.

What makes these stories funny and engaging is that we all know these children. They are our childhood friends, our neighbors, or our own children. I hope you have as much enjoyment reading about them as I have had in bringing them to you.

TOM BRANDON *has been a teacher, coach, and bus driver, and over the years he has served on a number of advisory councils. His awards include Teacher of the Year at his local school, the Coca-Cola Always Teaching Award, and the Steve Harvey Neighborhood Award.*

MR. BRANDON'S SCHOOL BUS

Family Outing

A first-grader approached the bus holding a small stuffed rabbit, a Mickey Mouse, and a toy cell phone. As I opened the door he said, "These are the little ones, and I'm keeping an eye on them today." He then looked down at them and said, "You guys are killing me!"

He seated himself, and them, and told them he was going to talk to me, but he would be keeping an eye on them. He showed me his phone and said, "If you don't mind I need to call my girlfriend."

It was definitely a woman on the other end. I could tell by the tone of the conversation. He started, "Yes, I'm on the bus, and I have the little ones with me. Yes, yes, yes, okay, yes, yes hun, okay, talk to you later."

Then he proceeded to call his buddy, Bob. "Hey, Bob. What you doing? . . . I'm on the bus with the little ones . . . Yes, I've got to keep an eye on them today . . . Yes, it's their first time to ride the bus, but they're doing all right."

I'm not sure if this information about the little ones messed up a hunting trip or guys' night on the town, but the next thing he said was, "Bob, don't you hang up on me."

He looked at me, shrugged his shoulders, and said, "I'll have to call him back later."

You never know when the burden of responsibility will be thrust upon you.

Where the Buffalo Roam

School bus route pickups start early and lend themselves to seeing some beautiful sunrises.

On such a morning, I had made several stops and was exiting a neighborhood. I eased the bus around a corner and brought it to a stop at the intersection. The bus was facing toward the rising sun and there, silhouetted against the sky, was a mother buffalo and her calf.

I could not help but pause and contemplate the beauty of God's creation. Feeling kindly toward all men, I prepared to move on when an excited voice from behind me called, "Mr. Brandon, he just threw up."

Looking in the mirror, I saw the offender peer over the seat with his little red face and watery eyes. He cleared his throat and said, "Mr. Brandon, what's for breakfast?"

Charles Dickens once penned, "It was the best of times, it was the worst of times . . ." So it was.

Life's Priority List

One morning, a second-grader with a rather distressed look on his face approached me. He said he needed to change seats.

So I inquired, "Why?" He took a quick look around, leaned forward, and whispered, "The person next to me keeps hitting me in my, my"—he took another look around—"my kumbayahs."

On life's list of important things to know, at least in the top five should be, "If your kumbayahs are ever in danger . . . move."

In a Pickle with the Law

The second-grader leaned forward, pointed to the side of the road, and said, "Mr. Brandon, you see that spot right there? My mom got stopped by the police there."

I wasn't sure if I should ask why, but my curiosity was relieved when he continued, "She was speeding. Well, she was really mad at the dog for fart'n in the car. You do not want to be around that dog after she's been eat'n hot pickles."

He paused and I gave him a nod of understanding. He continued, "They do the same thing to me but I wait till I go outside. I can bring you some hot pickles if you want."

How could I refuse an offer like that? The next day, he was standing at the bus stop with a quart of homemade hot pickles in each hand. I'm afraid I may have violated Ethics Law by accepting them.

Oh, he was right; they will work on you.

Charlie

Each of us has our daily routines. I try to leave the school each morning at the same time, each student expecting me at their familiar time.

Most mornings I pass the same cars that are also keeping their appointed schedules. There is the red car that I always meet going south as I go north. She always passes with a friendly wave and a warm smile. There is always that car with a Tennessee tag that flies past as if they are trying to qualify for the Daytona 500.

The routines continue with the children. There are three energetic boys that are always running around pushing and shoving each other as they wait for the bus. There are the procrastinators who always wait till the last minute to run to the bus from the house. Those putting on their shoes on the porch, so you will see them and not go off and leave them. The mother, in her well worn housecoat, who sticks her arm out the door and holds up one finger as if it were a flare to signal that her children will again take longer than anyone else on the route to get to the bus.

Then there is the daily routine of Charlie. When I stop to pick up one second-grader, Charlie is there to greet his master as he runs from the house to the bus. In the afternoon Charlie, is there again to greet him as he gets off the bus. Rain or shine, Charlie is a constant.

One morning as the second-grader emerged from the house, Charlie was excitedly wagging his little stubby tail so hard that it was shaking his entire body. You couldn't help but smile and feel a little chuckle in your heart. I didn't know goats could wag their tails like that.

Twins

Sisters, ages four and five who look very, very much alike, got on the bus, looked at me, and said in almost perfect unison, "We are not twins today. We are not twins tomorrow. We have different coats. We have different book bags and different hair bows."

Defensively, I said, "I never said you were twins."

They growled back, "Other people have been calling us twins, and if it keeps up there's going to be trouble. Somebody's going to get whipped!" Then once more in perfect unison they said, "WE ARE NOT TWINS!"

I feel sorry for anyone who uses the T-word in front of them.

Meow

With Pop-Tarts in hand, the pre-K student struggled up the steps to the bus. He looked at the package of Pop-Tarts and then at me and asked, "Can I eat these? I didn't have time this morning."

Well, the bus rules strictly forbid eating or drinking on the bus so I looked into his little innocent face and said, "Sure, but I better not find any crumbs on the floor of my bus."

With a grin on his face he started down the aisle to find a place to sit. Within a few minutes he was back at my elbow, "Mr. Brandon, I don't think I can eat these without getting a few crumbs on the floor."

"I understand," I told him. "But be careful and don't get too many." Later he was back with a Pop-Tart in hand and said, "Here you go, Mr. Brandon, you can have this one."

Not being a Pop-Tart fan I was not particularly interested, but I assumed it was an offering of gratitude for letting him eat the other one on the bus, knowing that most likely there was a small mountain of Pop-Tart crumbs on the floor.

As he handed me the Pop-Tart he added, "It's a super hero Pop-Tart."

I looked at it, and sure enough, there was Catwoman. I might have been able to turn down a Pop-Tart at any other time, but a Catwoman Pop-Tart, I don't think so. I think you could market mud pies if they had a picture of Catwoman on them. You put Catwoman on a Pop-Tart and that thing comes out of the package hot, no toaster needed.

As we pulled onto the school grounds he was once again at my side, waiting to get off the bus. Knowing that students are supposed to wait till the bus has come to a complete stop before they line up, several of the students told him he should sit down. His reply made clear that I had been a pawn in a web of graft and corruption.

He said to them, "It's okay, I gave him a Pop-Tart." It turned out the Pop-Tart was a payoff, a bribe; my good reputation had been compromised for a place in the front of the line.

Now the other students addressed me, "Mr. Brandon, he needs to sit down. We haven't stopped yet." I turned and looked at the driver's side window where I had carefully stood a Pop-Tart.

Looking back at me was Catwoman. Memories of Julie Newmar and Lee Meriwether flashed through my head, and I said, "It's okay, he gave me a Pop-Tart."

As they say, every man has his price.

Tag, You're It

There was a squeal from the brakes as the bus came to a stop in front of the house. As if in response, a shriek came from the house as a kindergartener burst out the door and ran to the bus waving her arms erratically in the air.

Close behind was her second-grader brother swinging his book bag over his head with one arm and the other arm was just waving around wildly. Every other step was a jump in the air.

Even though the door to the house had been closed, I know, I know I heard a voice say, "Tag, you're it."

Not My Angel

While taking children home after school, I noticed a car behind me that was very erratic in its movements. Concerned about such a vehicle following the bus too closely, I watched in the mirror to see if I could tell what the matter was.

I recognized the driver as a mother I had talked to earlier in the day. Her son had been put off the bus for his refusal to stay seated. She had, quite adamantly, told me that I was wrong and had judged her child too harshly.

The erratic movements of the car were from her

trying to get hold of her child, who was in the back seat jumping from side to side like a rabbit.

Mom, I think you'll find he was just excited and misunderstood.

Young Apprentice

We have all had a question asked of us to which we believe the answer should be very obvious, and in spite of our better judgement often answer in a very sarcastic way to show the foolishness of the question. I myself have been accused of engaging in such activity.

I was driving down the road and a second-grader—you know him as "Hot Pickle Boy"— asked me, "So what are you doing?" In a tone fitting for such a question, I replied, "I'm waterskiing. What are you doing?" Without hesitation, and in the same tone, he said, "I'm driving the boat."

I couldn't have been prouder.

Consequences

A normally cheerful student boarded the bus with his hat turned backwards and a disgruntled look on his face. As he sat there, he mumbled some rather grumpy remarks to those that were around him, who in turn looked back at him with puzzled looks wondering what they had done.

It looked as if this situation would continue to deteriorate. It was time for "Bad Attitude Intervention." I called his name, and he turned his furrowed brow toward me. "First things first," I started. "I believe the first step to making this a better day would to be to turn that hat around so that you look like somebody who knows the front from back and not look like a hood."

He slowly complied with the request. "Okay, handsome young man, let's move to step number two." There was no smile on his face, but the frown had subsided somewhat.

"Now I want you to look at each of the friends seated around you and say something nice about each of them, and they will say something nice about you."

There was an exchange of pleasantries such as, "You're a good friend, I like your hat, you're funny, and you're nice." As they looked at each other they began to laugh, and all was ended in good humor. Believing all was well, I left them alone. Little did I know, the snowball of happiness that I had put in motion was continuing downhill and was about to end in disaster.

The first sign was on hearing the now happy young

man singing, "I'm a tap-dancing monkey, I'm a tap-dancing monkey." He had removed from his backpack an old-fashioned sock monkey, and it was dancing across the back of the seat.

The musical cabaret continued with a performance of "Watch me whip, whip, watch me nae, nae." There was a slight intermission with a discussion of what exactly was a nae.

Then the snowball crashed into the peaceful valley below with sock monkey performing "I came in like a wrecking ball." This is not something you want to see a sock monkey perform. It will crush and destroy precious sock monkey memories that you have cherished from your childhood.

Note to self: a frown and furrowed brow are much preferred to an explicit sock monkey dance.

One Man's Junk Is Another Man's . . .

Going down the road, a wide-eyed preschooler popped up holding up a small piece of trash and said, "Look what I found on the floor." I enthusiastically replied, "Oh, you sure are lucky to find that. Be sure and put that in your pocket because that's good luck."

He disappeared and came back up with another lucky

piece. So I encouraged him to keep that one also. Before you knew it, all the preschoolers and kindergarteners around him were looking for lucky pieces. It was like a modern-day gold rush.

At least a half a dozen kids went home with pockets full of luck. One was so lucky, he told me that he had to start putting them in his jacket pockets.

By the way, there was a spot on my bus that looked like a Hoover had gone over it.

Cosmic Alignment

One of the greatest joys of working in education is being present when the gears turn just right, the planets align, and everything clicks. The light bulb comes on for a student, and it all makes sense.

Such a moment happened for one young man on the bus, and I was blessed to have him share it with me. In a voice that rang with the pride of accomplishment, he said, "Hey, Mr. Brandon, manure and poop are the same thing."

Knowledge is power!

Spokesperson

It was just before daylight, and the sun had not quite graced the horizon. The second-grader came to the bus with his backpack thrown over one shoulder, a thumb under the strap holding it in place. In the other hand he carried his sunglasses. Yes, sunglasses. You know how the blinding glare of the sun can beat down on you as you ride a school bus before daybreak.

He paused at the steps, holding the sunglasses by one earpiece. He looked up at me, one eyebrow up, one down, and then flicked the glasses so the other earpiece swung gracefully out. Then ever so slowly, he slid them into place, every bit the man of mystery.

Oh, I get it. Not worn for practicality but for fashion purposes. He proceeded up the steps, paused at the mirror, took the glasses off, smoothed back his hair, and slowly slid them back on like a bad biker boy.

As he was seated I looked in the mirror to see him pull the glasses off again. He looked at me in the mirror and placed the glasses just so they sat on the lower part of his nose and the earpieces just touched the ears. As he continued to look at me over the top of the glasses, he placed one finger on the bridge of the glasses and slowly pushed them up his nose and into place with the "I don't want to be disturbed" move. With this being done, he placed his hands behind his head and leaned back in the seat in satisfaction.

The removing and replacing continued a number of times, using every model move he had ever seen on TV. He removed and replaced his sunglasses enough times, I am convinced, to have raised a blister on his ears. A trained model could not have demonstrated the merchandise better.

Then came the sales pitch. As another young man boarded the bus, he pulled the glasses off with one hand, tipped the ear pieces toward the young man in typical authority fashion and said, "Son, your daddy needs to get you a pair of sunglasses just like these. You can find them in the sporting goods section of Walmart." Then, in his ever so sophisticated fashion, he slid them back on.

I don't know if he is receiving any compensation, but I almost felt I needed a pair.

Changes

"Well," the young man said in a tone loud enough to gain the attention of those around him, "in a couple of weeks I'll be having another birthday and you know what that means." The students around him and myself waited to hear what that meant.

There was a pause, then all was revealed,

"I'll be having a birthday, and then it won't be but a few more years and I'll be going through puberty, and things will start happening." He definitely had my attention. He looked at the others and said, "Let me tell you about it."

I cleared my throat loud enough to get his attention, and he looked at me in the mirror. "There are some things that we do not share with younger children," I said. He frowned and nodded his head yes.

Then he looked at a second-grade girl seated in front of him and said, "Trust me, some changes are coming your way."

I cleared my throat again and shook my head no. So he changed tactics, paused for a moment, and said, "Mr. Brandon when did you grow that mustache?" I must have given him a disapproving look without realizing it, because before I could answer he said, "Come on, Mr. Brandon, give me a break here, big man is going through some changes."

Before I could reply, he continued. "I'm sure my older brothers will be good role models; they have already talked to me about"—I took a deep breath and gritted my teeth—"They have already talked to me about how to kick a football."

I hope that is the only step of puberty that we have to worry about at this time.

Staking a Claim

If they ever find an industrial use for mucus, I have a kindergartener on the bus that I'm making a claim on. When you hear someone sneeze on the bus followed by a number of screams, you know exactly who it was that sneezed. I just hand back the whole box of Kleenex and say, "Give me back what's left." Talk about a renewable resource. He just keeps on giving.

Counselor in the Making

A little red-headed first-grader said, "Mr. Brandon, did you know that my mom was in your class when she was little?"

"Yes, I did. And one of these days you will be old enough to be in my class just like your mom," I replied.

She continued, "Did you go to this school when you were a little boy?"

"No, I lived in another state. I lived in Oklahoma."

"You mean you had to move off and leave all your friends?" At this point in the conversation, I reached up to wipe something out of my eye. I felt a little hand patting me on the shoulder and then a soft voice said, "Are you crying, Mr. Brandon?"

At this same moment, we passed a cemetery and she said, "There are a lot of people out there. Do you miss your mom and dad?" I replied, "My mom and dad are still alive." A moment's hesitation and she tried another approach, "How about your grandma and grandpa?"

Then, the little hand returned to patting me and she said, "Mr. Brandon, do you get frustrated sometimes?"

I think her career path has already been chosen.

What Could Have Been

As the bus climbed the small hill approaching a rather challenging young man's house, no one was standing at the end of the drive. My breathing slowed and I gritted my teeth, trying to hold back the emotions.

I slowed the bus to a stop. Still no one. I fought back the dream of what the ride might be like. A few more seconds went by. Still no one.

The sun came through the trees. The wheat in the fields was golden, and the birds began to sing. My heart leapt with joy. My foot moved from the brake to the accelerator.

In that very moment of delight, the front door flew

open and out he ran, followed by his little brother. I looked to the heavens and said, "Now, Lord, that was just mean."

Sir Isaac

Newton is well known for his three "Laws of Motion." Less well known are Brandon's "Laws of Buses."

1. Law of Speed and Digestion: The faster you need to get off the bus and do something else, the better the chance someone will throw up, requiring you to spend a little more quality time on the bus. Also related is the fact that the sicker a rider is, the further his house or school will be.

2. Law of Behavior and Attendance: The more discipline problems a student is involved in, the greater the chance they will have perfect attendance. This law has proven equally true in the classroom.

3. Law of Directionality: When driving an unfamiliar route, the first student to get off the bus knows the route best. The student who gets off last not only does not know the route, but does not even know his or her own address.

Lookin' Good

Dressed to the T's and all grins, it had to be kindergarten graduation. As they came to the bus, they wanted you to see how dressed up they were, so at the top of the steps each paused for inspection.

A little girl, in curls done by her personal-hairdresser Mom, had to show me her new dress, the latest in fashion in north Alabama, new shoes normally reserved for church, and earrings just like a grown-up. She said, "Mr. Brandon, I bet you didn't even recognize me."

One little boy showed me his new tie and even bent over to let me smell his hair gel. I said, "Man, you look sharp today. You getting married or are you preaching today?"

He just flashed a missing-half-my-teeth smile and said, "I'm all tucked in and lookin' good."

New Grade, New Experiences

Mr. Mucus got on the bus all excited about going to the first grade. First, he patted me on the shoulder and reassured me that I was still his buddy. I looked to make sure nothing sticky was left behind.

Then he told me how things would be different in the first grade. He said, "In kindergarten, we had cubbies to put our stuff in, and in your room they have lockers. In first-grade, we have hookers."

I was hoping he just meant hooks, but just in case, I made a trip past the first-grade rooms that day.

Don't Shoot

Anyone who has been around Hot Pickle Boy for any length of time knows that he is one of the greatest untapped resources for natural gas in the United States. Trust me, when he steps up beside you, grins, and says, "I'm fix'n to pull the trigger on this thing," it's not going to be pleasant.

Academic Excellence

Walmart has nothing on our bus. We also have our own greeter. One morning as other students boarded the bus, a first-grader said, "Welcome to Walnut Grove Usafurtee." "You-say-fur-tee?" I replied. "What's a Usafurtee?"

"You know, like Alabama Usafurtee."

"You mean Alabama University?" I said.

"Yes, Walnut Grove Usafurtee," he repeated.

We have always strived to increase our academic

excellence at Walnut Grove, and apparently we had moved up several levels. I understood all we needed to make it official was a contract for collegiate wear.

Rumor had it there was already an NCAA investigation into our athletic program for possible recruiting violations involving a new bicycle and preferential seating on the school bus.

Random Thoughts—World Peace

We live in an amazing world!

Though I do not consider myself old, I have had the privilege of being around for a number of years. In those years I have seen many amazing changes.

I have seen the day when the best thing you could purchase for your child's education was a set of encyclopedias that took up a substantial amount of space. Now we just Google it. I have watched all three channels on a black and white TV while serving as my father's remote control. Now you can miss an hour-long program that you wanted to watch on your 72-inch high-definition television, because it took so long to go through the 900 available channels.

As a teacher I have gone home with my hands covered with chalk dust and purple ink from mimeographed papers. Now I have a printer right in my classroom and an interactive board that is attached to my computer that will electronically write in any color of my choosing.

As a bus driver I have driven manual-shift buses that had exposed metal bars around the thinly padded seats and were cold and rattled as you went down the road. Now my bus has an automatic transmission, air shocks, tinted windows, heating and air conditioning front and back, radio, and CD player. I don't even have to reach over to open the door for students—I have an air-operated door activated with a button on the steering wheel.

Forgive the nostalgia, but this past week I was introduced to what has to be history's greatest advancement.

In my lifetime, I have visited a number of outhouses. Many of you know what I speak of. I have visited one- and two-holers whose seats were worn smooth over the years so one would never get a splinter. It was always questionable what you would find in them to "clean" yourself with after the job was finished. I once used toilet paper in Russia that I believe I got a paper cut from.

But my daughter and five-month-old grandson often stay with us during the work week. With a baby in the house there are numerous diaper changes, and with that came the moist, flushable wipes. That alone should have some recognition.

Then my daughter brought in a device that I believe given time and the right consideration could change the course of the world. It is sized to hold a package of wipes and then—be still, my beating heart—you plug it in and it warms, yes, warms the wipes. Not only are they moist, for a better job, but *warm*. Oh, what a blessed invention to be introduced to in the chilly month of December!

With one of these in every world leader's bathroom, how could they not come out with a good feeling toward all mankind?

Forgive me, Leonardo da Vinci. Move over, Thomas Edison. Why has this not made world headlines? I have never been one to spend a lot of time in the royal chamber, but if my family needs me in cold future months, I can tell them now where to look first.

I may even have decided what room to move the set of encyclopedias to.

The Motivator

All of us have seen the man at the airport with his orange flashlights directing the planes to their appropriate places.

One morning, I looked in the mirror to see a young man with a glow stick in each hand, waving them forward as he called out, "Straight ahead Mr. Brandon, straight ahead. Let's keep this thing rolling. You're doing great. You're doing great."

When he gave me that extra nod of approval, I admit I felt pretty good about myself.

Multi-tool

Mr. Mucus came to the bus with a cloth over his hand. I opened the bus door and he said, "Presto!" as he yanked the cloth off his hand.

So I inquired, "What you got there?"

"Well," he started, "this is my ol' rag. You can use it for magic tricks. You can clean things with it. And I can use it to wipe my nose if I need to."

After he was seated, I looked in the mirror and saw him wiping down the back of the seat.

Then he looked up at me, put the rag across his arm, and said, "Can I interest you in a cold drink this morning, sir?" I asked for tea and was promptly served.

As I approached the next house I heard, "Great, two more customers."

The ol' rag was being used as a hat before we reached school.

I can see it now. Introducing *My Ol' Rag* by Mr. Mucus.

Swiss Army Knives have got nothing on *My Ol' Rag*!

We may have to run this by the promotions department.

Open Invitation

As I was picking up the Twins That Are Not Twins, their large dog in the backyard was putting up quite a commotion.

They got on the bus and told me, "That's our dog Brownie. He really doesn't like people. If we turned him loose, he would probably jump on you. Then he would grab your arm and maybe tear it off, and then start on your legs." And without a pause they said, "Do you want to go see him?"

Pass. Brownie is best admired from a distance.

Profiling

There is a true rite of passage that all children go through, especially little boys. Usually an older brother, or *that* uncle—you know who he is—who helps by taking care of the finer details of your child's education that professional educators and yourself somehow overlook.

Such is the time-honored art of making gas passing

noises by blowing on your arm. Well, from behind me I heard someone demonstrating their newly acquired talents, and doing it quite well.

I looked into the mirror to find the music makers. As I scanned the seats, the obvious choice was the Three Stooges: a first-grader and two kindergarteners, eagerly engaged in being boys by whacking each other in the head with pieces of paper.

"Boys," I said. "Quit." After a short time of silence, the sound started again. "Boys, I said quit." There was a pause, then another loud vibrating bugle. I responded in a firm fatherly voice. "Boys, did you hear what I said?"

They looked at me, pointed across the aisle, and said, "Okay, we will. But would you tell those girls to quit making those farting sounds?"

Whereupon two cute little girls peeked over the seat at me and grinned.

The Young and the Restless

The kindergartener got on the bus with his usual "I'm excited about the day" grin. He eagerly searched the bus for his best buddy, and there he was, barely able to see over the seat, waving his arms so he could be spotted.

He went back, both of them all smiles. As he prepared

to sit down, he looked across the aisle and there she was, a different kind of kindergartener. The kind with long, blond, curly hair with ribbons and a smile that makes your heart do funny things.

He looked at his buddy, back at her, back at his buddy, and did the only reasonable thing someone with a Y chromosome could do—he sat down by her. They were all grins and giggles.

His buddy, with a knot in his stomach, slid over by the window to ride by himself. A few miles down the road, I looked in the mirror to check on the progress of young love, only to see the little girl leaning against the window with a frown on her face. It didn't take long to see why.

Her first conquest was sitting on the edge of the seat talking to his best buddy across the aisle.

You find out early they're great for grins and giggles, but for serious paper wad throwing, paper airplane flying, and crawling under the seat exploration, there's nothing like your best buddy.

Stay the Course

A second-grader approached the bus with a red straw stuck on the end of a pencil. I could tell by the way he was holding it that it was no longer a straw and pencil in his mind but some other kind of utensil.

He stepped on the bus and told me it was his magic wand. He then proudly showed the others around him the pencil and straw—I mean—magic wand.

Then, without their consent, he promptly started turning everyone around him into frogs, lizards, and other animals.

Having no appreciation for the magical arts, the Twins Who Are Not Twins started screaming, "It's just a pencil and straw. It's just a pencil and straw."

Not dissuaded, he continued on his merry round of reducing the population of the bus to small helpless creatures. Which, for most, was actually an improvement.

Grief

I was reminded of the familiar quote from Alfred Lord Tennyson, "'Tis better to have loved and lost than never to have loved at all."

All who know Mr. Mucus know he approaches all things with zest and excitement as if that very minute was the greatest time of his life. But it was a much subdued and quiet Mr. Mucus who approached.

With bowed head and faint voice, he said, "Mr. Brandon, did you hear the news?" Having shared in the lives of my riders over the years, I prepared to listen.

Because of his tone of voice, I expected the worst, already feeling a heaviness in my own heart. "Did you hear they are closing the Ryan's restaurant? My father told me about it last night."

I gathered myself and in an equally hushed tone said, "I know, I heard that, too. What are you going to do?"

I could hear a small quiver in his voice as he said, "I don't know..." He paused to gain control of his emotions. "I have to admit when my father told me, I cried a little bit. I had a hard time concentrating on my homework after that. So last night we went to Golden Corral. As we were eating my father looked across the table at me and said, 'It's just not the same.'"

Then, with feet and heart that seemed too heavy to lift, he moved silently back to his seat. True love. Great are the rewards, deep are the sorrows.

Just Won't Stop

The first-grader boarded the bus, and I watched in the rearview mirror for him to be seated before I pulled away.

He paused in front of a seat and started jumping around. I asked what the problem was and why he was not seated.

"Well, Mr. Brandon," he started. "It's my shoes. They're dancey today and I can't get them to stop." He must have been right, because even after he sat down, his shoes just kept right on moving.

I imagine that dancey shoe days are pretty good days.

Pachyderm Problems

Having an elephant with you can cause a number of problems if you have not planned things out.

I was surprised by a first-grader who asked, "Mr. Brandon, do you have an extra diaper?" Not realizing that this would be a need on the route that day, I was caught short-handed and had to say no.

He explained that he had already pulled the poopy diaper off of his elephant and needed a clean one to put on. That seemed reasonable after he told me the elephant was only two months old.

Next, he got in an argument about the age of the elephant with a much wiser third-grader who was explaining that the elephant's size was not realistic for a two-month-old elephant, and we know third-graders are known for their expertise on elephants.

Of course, I was called in to verify the age since he had told me earlier, and bus drivers are known for their expertise in judging the age of elephants.

Things calmed down when he took out a book and started reading to the elephant about sharks. Apparently elephants are interested in sea life.

So when traveling with an elephant, be sure to carry 1. Diapers, 2. Documentation of age, and 3. Plenty of reading material, preferably about sea creatures.

Hunting?

Mr. Mucus was overflowing with excitement as he told Hot Pickle Boy and me that he was now a Scout Boy. He said that Scout Boys go camping, hiking, and hunting. One of the first things they were going to do in the Scout Boys was go fish hunting.

Hot Pickle Boy, being the refined redneck that he is, took a deep breath when Mr. Mucus said "fish hunting." He then explained the differences in hunting and fishing, and that normally you use a pole for fishing and a gun for hunting, but if you used a gun for fishing it was still called fishing.

At this point, we had reached an intersection and Mr. Mucus veered from the conversation to inform me to turn left. I told him thanks, and that without his help I was sure I would get lost. Mr. Mucus replied, "You're welcome. Rule number 200 of the Scout Boys is "Always go the right direction."

He then asked if he could push the button to make the lights come on when we stopped to pick up the next student. I informed him that rule number 250 of the Scout Boys was "Don't push the bus driver's buttons," which is not that difficult to do on some days. He seemed to be okay with that.

With him that fired up to follow the Scout Boy rules, I was thinking I would tell him about Scout Boy rule number 68—"Bring your bus driver a chocolate donut."

Engaging the Enemy

As the volume between two boys started to increase, it was evident that they were in a rather heated argument.

The battle of words raged on, and the ultimate verbal weapon was unsheathed. The "Your Momma" assault had started.

The "Your Momma" insult is a powerful force and not to be used casually. In the case of such lethal weaponry, one needs to be trained in its proper usage and the appropriate time for its deployment.

After several vicious exchanges, I called a ceasefire to explain. The "Your Momma" attack was not the weapon to use in this instance since . . . they were brothers. Not step-brothers, but brothers.

I left them looking at each other with puzzled expressions on their faces. It was a lot to think about.

Gifts

We have all received a gift that we realized was just for show, or from givers who felt obligated, or from those who tried to justify the skimpiness of the gift by saying, "It's the thought that counts."

Well, not when we can tell there was not much thought put into it. With that being said, I was pleased and honored with the gift that two small boys dumped into my hand when they boarded the bus. It showed thought and effort.

The question is, what do you do with a handful of roly polies?

One Foggy Morning

The fog was so heavy that it muted even the sound of the children on the bus. There were questions about the fog—the usual where, when, and why—and even these were given in hushed tones.

One concerned small girl asked if I thought we would make it to school. As I drove on, it was almost silent as the students' gazes strained to pierce the fog and see what was ahead.

When it grew even quieter, I threw up a hand and yelled, "Ahhhhhhhhh."

Payback is a wonderful thing. There was a lack of breathing from the students for a number of seconds.

The Claw

The doors opened and big brother hurried onto the bus. Little brother turned for one last embrace from mom, which is not uncommon. It then turned from an embrace to a clinch. He then became a preschool cocklebur with all of his little spines buried in the folds of his mother's clothing.

With great effort, she slowly peeled him off. You could almost hear Velcro was being ripped away.

She dangled him at arm's length, making sure he could not make contact with her and reattach himself. She placed him as far up the bus steps as her arms would allow.

Then, the bus driver's arm reached out like the claw on the machine at the county fair. Grab and miss, moving target, an adjustment, another grab, and then contact.

The claw closed on the backpack and unceremoniously lifted the preschooler into the air.

Little feet dangling, he was deposited in the aisle to find a place to be seated. The door closed, and the bus moved toward whatever games of skill and chance awaited at the next stop.

Food for Thought

To small children, these are the facts: 1. You are an adult. 2. You drive a big yellow bus. 3. Therefore, you are an authority and can be called on to answer any question.

After some discussion about that cereal with the lion on the front, it was determined that it was a tiger and this question was posed: "Mr. Brandon, if a tiger took a bite out of me, how big of a bite could he get?"

Trying to be a factual science teacher, I replied, "Well, he would probably grab your head, and his mouth is big enough to put your whole head in. Then his teeth would go right through your skull."

As if to discourage any child-eating tigers in the area, he started hitting himself in the head and said, "I don't know. My head is pretty hard." After about four blows to the head, I agreed and let him stagger back to his seat.

No, he's not tiger-food material.

Some Assembly Required

As I approached the house, there was no sign of the little girl who usually got on at that address, but I stopped anyway. After waiting a reasonable time, I started to drive off.

Before I could pull away, the front door flew open. Out came the mother carrying her daughter. I opened the door, smiled, and said "Good morning."

The mother stepped on the bus, and without a word or a smile, put the little girl in my lap, handed me her socks and shoes, turned, and walked off the bus.

Some people just aren't morning people.

Go, Granny, Go

It was 6:30 a.m. and dark, and as I eased around the narrow corner of a neighborhood street Hot Pickle Boy said, "Look out for the little old lady in the wheel chair."

My first reaction was, what kind of crazy story is he starting with today? At that same time, out of the corner of my eye, what should appear but a little old lady in a wheel chair on the side of the road?

Caught a little off guard I said, "A little old lady should not be in the road in a wheel chair in the dark." To which Mr. Mucus replied, "She should have been on roller skates."

Safety First

A first-grader had to tell me about his new gadget. "Mr. Brandon, my Dad got me a robot hand to pick things up with. You can pick up broken glass and other dangerous things with it so you won't get hurt."

"Right."

"I'm using it to pick up my underwear so I can smell them and tell if they are dirty or clean."

The sad thing is that everyone reading this has sniffed a pair of drawers at one time or another, maybe even this morning.

There's Always Something to Smile About

Well, the worst thing that could happen to a bus driver happened. While I was stopped to drop off a child, an SUV slammed into the back of the bus.

As you can imagine, there was a lot of excitement. After the initial shock, the students did great. One student told me he had never been in a wreck before and this was exciting.

Seeing one little girl seated alone and very quiet, I asked her if she was all right. She just looked at me, smiled, and said, "Wow!"

As the EMTs were checking on the kids, I turned

around to survey the whole thing. Who is looking at me with a grin from ear to ear but Mr. Mucus, who gave me thumbs up. I was asked a thousand questions as the EMTs worked, "What are they doing?" followed by "What are they doing now?"

Everyone made it home okay. Those who rode the bus the next morning all had to tell me what happened, as if I wasn't there. There was an argument from one boy who wanted to know why they didn't interview him for the news instead of that little girl because he could have done a better job.

With all the talk going on as we drove down the road, the bus hit a rather large pothole which caused a loud bang.

At any other time, this would not even have been noticed, but on this morning it brought complete silence.

Then a voice hollered, "Hey, Mr. Brandon, you trying to kill us again?" Then everybody burst out laughing.

Mr. Mucus shouted, "Mr. Brandon, you're the man."

I guessed we were all okay and back to normal, or as normal as can be a bus load of nutty kids and a bus driver who is questionable himself.

Fashion Trends from the Garden

We know how fashion-minded young ladies can be. So it was no surprise to see approaching the bus a thin, rather tall, fifth-grade girl wearing all the latest brightly colored fashions. Including a headband that she had pulled down over her head and then pushed back up causing her hair to stand straight up.

Her walk let you know that she had it all going on.

As she stepped onto the bus, she paused, then continued down the aisle as if on the runway in a Parisian fashion show.

A kindergartener took one look and said, "You look like a piece of broccoli."

I hope the shaking of my shoulders did not give away how hard I was silently laughing, but it was the perfect description.

As we approached the school thirty minutes later, I could still hear her mumbling to herself, "He said I looked like a piece of broccoli."

Random Thoughts—Summer Breeze

"If it were a snake it would have bit you" was a phrase often used by my father.

He would send us after something he needed. When

time passed and we had not returned, he would show up. We would report that we were unable to find the item. He would then reach just a few feet from where we were standing and retrieve the item. Truly, if it had been a snake it would have bitten us.

Often in life, it seems, things are right there, yet we do not see them.

Getting older is a good example. All the signs were there, I just wanted to ignore them. Age was trying to make itself known, but I refused to see it.

My truck tried to tell me. Yes, my truck. I looked down to read a message that had come up on the dashboard: "Your turn indicator has been left on." How long does your turn signal have to be left on until even the truck says, "Hey, old man, turn your blinkers off."

The next evening, I had an opportunity to pass on that feeling that comes when you feel age creeping up.

My wife came home from work and pulled off her shoes, complaining about how much her feet were hurting. We sat for a few minutes, then got up to head for her mother's house to fix supper.

Since we were just going to her mom's house, she said, "You know, my feet are hurting so bad I think I'll just wear my house shoes."

She slid those fluffy things on.

Not being one to let opportunity pass, I started with the "Come on, Granny" jokes. I asked if she needed me to get her walking stick. Then, taking her by the arm, I said, "Come on, Momma, let's shuffle on out to the truck."

On the way to the truck, I delivered every old-person joke and innuendo that I could think of. She accepted them all with her usual smile. I opened her door and helped her into the truck as I would any elderly lady.

As I was about to close her door, she smiled and said, "Gramps, before you get in, you might want to zip your pants."

Yes, the signs are often there but ignored until brought to our attention by a dear loved one or a gentle breeze.

True Confessions

Sometimes people, including students, find themselves needing to share information that will ease the burden of knowledge that rests so heavily upon their shoulders.

These confessions can burst without apparent relevance into the middle of any conversation, or they can spontaneously erupt in a moment of quiet.

One day Hot Pickle Boy shared, "Mr. Brandon, Life Savers and toothpaste do not go together."

Another time, Mr. Mucus quietly confided, "Mr. Brandon, my favorite number is five, I am . . . well . . . a little chubby and would be hard to fit in a small microwave and I once shot a man out of a cannon."

Since confession is good for the soul, I knew I had at least two students walking a little easier.

I myself came away a little concerned that a child knew his size in comparison to a microwave oven.

Just Dirt and Grass

Throughout the world, facial recognition software is now being used to identify people the way we used to from their fingerprints. Regardless of how well facial recognition works, it cannot compare with bus drivers' ability to identify small students just by the tops of their heads.

About halfway through the route one afternoon, I spotted in my rearview mirror the top of a head that I didn't recognize. I did recognize the top of the head next to it, so I called out, "Charlie, who is that sitting next to you?"

A little face with a big grin popped up and said, "That's Luke."

So then I called out, "Luke, what are you doing on my bus?"

Another face with a big grin popped up and said, "I don't know."

"Well, what do you usually do after school?"

"I don't know."

"Are you a car rider; do you stay in after-school daycare?"

"I don't know."

"When you ride a bus, whose bus do you ride, Mr. Berry's?"

"No, I ride Mr. Brandon's."

"Do you mean Mr. Page?"

"No, I ride Mr. Brandon's."

"Luke, I'm Mr. Brandon, and you don't ride this bus. What is your address? Where do you live?"

You guessed it—"I don't know."

His grin had by now slid somewhat off his face. Before I could reach for the two-way radio, a voice came over the radio: "School to Mr. Brandon."

I was pretty sure what this was going to be about, so I answered, "Hey, I've got a Luke here."

Response: "Do you want his parents to meet you at school or do you want to take him home?"

"Well, the problem would be this, Luke doesn't know where he lives and neither do I."

The school gave me an approximate location, and

when I had dropped off all the other kids, we headed that way. Luke promised that if I got close to his house he could show me which one it was. To reassure me, he pointed at a barn and said, "We must be close, I think I've seen that barn before. You'll know my house when you see it because we don't have a real driveway, just dirt and grass, not even rocks."

Well, it wasn't long before we found a driveway with just dirt and grass, no rocks, and he got off with a smile on his face.

All was well.

Actually, the Luke episode had turned out to be easy . . . compared to the time the little boy told me his was "the house with the horse in the field next to it."

What a Difference Spelling Makes

One question you can count on Mr. Mucus to ask each morning: "Mr. Brandon, what's for breakfast?"

Sometimes I tell him the truth and sometimes I make stuff up, trying to make it so ridiculous that he will know I am messing with him.

It doesn't always work.

There was the morning he became afraid that the porcupine pancakes I had mentioned would get caught in his throat. On another occasion I said, "Liver sandwiches."

He called back, "It better not be cat liver or I will throw up."

While multiple ideas were running through my head of why he would think about cat liver, another student cleared up my confusion when he told Mr. Mucus, "Not litter . . . liver."

The Agency

As the second-grader approached the bus, he had a folded piece of cardboard, obviously a cell phone, up against his ear. As I opened the door, he brought his conversation to an end with, "Yes, yes, that's good. I will talk to you later."

He snapped shut the cardboard—I mean, phone—and said, "The Agency. You know I'm a spy."

I was sure I heard spy music start up in the background. Not wanting to blow his cover I said, "If you're a spy, should you be telling me this?"

He leaned in and whispered, "I'm Double Oh Oh. I have a microchip in one shoe and a blow dryer in the other shoe."

The microchip made sense; I'm sure a spy would need one in a lot of different circumstances. But I must admit the blow dryer threw me until I realized how handsome and sophisticated spies always look. I guess you would need a readily available blow dryer.

Just as our conversation was getting interesting, his phone must have rung because he said, "Excuse me, I have to get this."

He answered his phone with, "Yes, Dear, I'm on my way to work . . . Do we have to talk about this now? . . . Can't we talk about this tomorrow? Okay, goodbye."

He hung up, looked at me, and affirmed the obvious: "The wife."

I don't know what she said, but it seemed to have taken the starch out of him. He dropped his head and said in a somewhat muted tone, "I'll be sitting back here if you need me."

He didn't stay downcast for long. In a few minutes he announced to the bus he was ordering jetpacks for everybody so they could fly to school. He got back on the phone and when he got off announced to everyone, "They're on their way."

I guess he must have sensed some confusion among his fellow riders, which he tried to clear up by announcing, "Yes, I am a spy. Why else would a second-grader have so many gadgets?"

After this there was not much more activity on the

spy front, but as we neared school I heard him call out my name. I caught his eyes in my mirror and watched as he blew on one thumb, then the other thumb, slapped his hands together, then waved them over his head.

I'm sure this was some spy code. From the smile on his face it must have meant that all was well, mission completed.

Time Savers

After picking up the Twins That Are Not Twins, I always turn around and go back past their house. One morning as I turned around, one of them said, "Mr. Brandon, I have to use the bathroom bad. I don't think I can hold it all the way to school."

I asked, "Why didn't you go before you got on the bus?"

"Well, my sister was in there and she wouldn't hurry up."

Knowing that school was about forty minutes away, I asked, "If I stop back at your house, can you run in and use the bathroom real quick?"

She assured me she could, so I let her off the bus.

As she ran for the house, her sister said, "She'll be fast all right, because she don't never flush or wash her hands."

It's those pesky personal hygiene chores that cut into our valuable time.

The True Spirit

One morning a rider asked, "Mr. Brandon, do you know what the true spirit of Christmas is?"

Sensing a teaching moment, I replied, "Yes, I do, the true spirit of Christmas is seeing how many presents you can get for your bus driver."

He and a chorus chimed in: "No, Mr. Brandon, it's about being thankful."

I said, "Yes, thankful that we are able to buy a lot of presents for our bus driver."

"No, it's about being able to do things for the people who mean the most to you and that you love the most."

I started in with, "Yes, like—"

They interrupted with, "We know . . . like your bus driver."

My job was done.

The conversation then changed to what if we could hook up reindeer to the bus.

Disco on the Bus

After a few minutes on the bus your friend and mine, Mr. Mucus, pulled his head into his jacket and zipped it up so his head was inside. In a few moments he started yelling, "Go, go, run!"

The students around him asked what he was doing. He informed them that he was watching a ball game on his big screen TV. He continued to yell for his team until the game was over.

At this point there was a pause, and then he said, "All right," and started moving around in the seat in a circular motion. He must have been aware of the questioning eyes on him, and he replied from inside, "I've turned on the disco ball in the dance room."

He gyrated a number of times, the movements getting larger and larger until he hit his head a good lick on the seat in front of him. He fell back in the seat. Knowing that we were concerned, a voice from inside called out, "I'm not dead."

Then, "I think I'll go back to watching television."

It's All in the Details

A first-grade student boarded the bus, sat down, and said, "Mr. Brandon, why is it so chilly this morning?"

A quick thought ran through my head—maybe it's not so obvious to a first-grader.

I replied, "Because it's December."

He looked at me with a blank stare. I tried again, "Because it's winter."

His look remained the same, so I swung for the fences. "Because during this period of time the tilt of the earth's axis causes the northern hemisphere to be tilted away from the sun."

"Oh, so that's why," he replied.

Some people think on a higher level, even first-graders.

Proper Etiquette

We use titles or phrases such as Your Majesty, Your Highness, Sir, and Madame to address others to show honor or respect. Often, much can be accomplished when we take the time to be polite.

Yet sometimes we are caught in a situation where we are not exactly sure how to address or greet someone. When you're not sure, do not use uncertainty as an excuse not to show proper form. Go with what you know.

This lesson I learned from Mr. Mucus.

As students boarded one morning, he addressed each

by name with a courteous, "Good morning, Joe. Good morning, Alice."

This he continued at each stop until one student got on. Mr. Mucus paused, looked at him, and said, "Good morning, little child that I have never seen before."

Extra Effort

As Mr. Mucus boarded the bus, I said, "Kind of frosty out there this morning."

He replied, "That's why you got a D.J. on the bus."

Naturally I was at a complete loss for what that meant. I was unaware of a D.J. that was used exclusively for frosty weather, so I asked, "What's a D.J.?"

"It's a person that spins records so you can dance," he replied and threw his hands in several different directions. "By the way, I've learned some new hip-hop moves and will be giving some free lessons today." At this point he pulled off his jacket to show me his new Cub Scout T-shirt and explained to me that two fingers in the air means listen with your wolf ears. Before he put his jacket back on he said, "Mr. Brandon, do you know what my jacket says?"

I gave the back of his jacket a quick glance and said, "I don't know, what does it say?"

He looked it up and down, and I heard him mutter, "What does this thing say?"

Giving up, he turned it back to me and said, "Come on man, you've got to try harder."

Sometimes a little extra effort is what is needed.

Promotional Gimmick

Mr. Mucus boarded the bus with "Yessssss, the school bus."

I knew he was primed to go. It wasn't long before I saw him in the mirror putting a long piece of tape under his nose. He caught me looking and said, "What?—it's a moustache." He then properly interpreted my look of you-have-got-to-be-kidding-me and continued, "I got it free with my cappuccino."

The first thought that flashed through my mind was that I had been driving through this neighborhood for a number of years, how had I missed a Starbucks? Was it hidden behind the barn on the corner? Was it down by the stock pond where the horses water, or was it near where I often slow down to let chickens cross the road? Secondly, this was a promotion I had not even heard of.

I refocused and he gave me a thumbs-up assuring that

he was self-confident in his new look. But he must have had a change of heart because before we got to school, he had torn the tape in half, put a piece under each eye, and announced that he was a football player.

Personally I think he should have stuck with the mustache, though they do tend to catch cappuccino foam.

Looks Like a Job for a Bus Driver

Each day I dropped a little first-grader off at a community store. His grandmother and mother lived next-door and ran the store. It was the kind of store where if you don't have enough money for a pack you can buy a single cigarette.

Each day when I pulled up to let him off, Bubba, his little brother, would run out in his underwear to wave at the bus and greet his brother.

One day while passing through the neighborhood after my route was over, I stopped in for a snack. The boys were running around playing in the store. The mother said, "Oh, Mr. Brandon, I'm so glad that you came by. I could sure use your help."

Well, if you have ever been in this kind of situation, it's quite humbling. Knowing that she was a single mother, with no male influence in the household to help with the boys, and doing her best to make a living and do what she could for her family, I was a little taken aback that she would confide in me. But I stepped closer and said, "I'll be glad to. How can I help?"

She looked at the boys. She looked back at me. She leaned forward and in a quiet voice said, "I need you to talk to Bubba." She then told me what she needed me to talk to Bubba about.

So while sitting on the steps drinking RC Colas and sharing a bag of peanuts, Bubba and I discussed why he needed to start wearing pants if he was going to start school next year.

Not sure if my reasoning was all that sound, but I gave it a shot.

Everyone Is Invited

He boarded the bus with a handful of papers, stuck them in my face, and said, "Mr. Brandon, what do you think?"

It was about five pages of scribbles but by his tone of voice, I knew I was being shown something important. So I shook my head and said, "Looks good, looks real good. How about explaining it to me?"

So he sat down and explained the plans for his

"Summer Club—it's a club where you just hang out for the summer and have a good time."

He asked me how to spell "pull" and I said, "*Pull*, like you pull open a door?"

"No, like you jump in a *pull*."

"Oh, you mean *pool*."

"Yes, *pull*."

"P-O-O-L," I replied.

He went on, "We are just going to hang around the pull all summer and have a good time."

I thought this was very ambitious since they did not currently have a pull. Then he started making a list of all the food and drinks they would need, and he solicited the help of a third-grader for the spelling.

Next came the good news. He started explaining who all was invited to be a part of the "Summer Club." He named brothers, sisters, cousins, grandpa, grandma, all the way out to uncles and aunts.

According to him it would start Spring 4:30.

I hoped they would have the pull by then.

Affairs of the Heart

Oh, how February brings out the love bug! What to say, what to do?

Two second-grade boys were discussing how one of them had been practicing to kiss his girlfriend on Valentine's Day by kissing a stuffed deer head at home. Well, another second-grader came to me and asked, "Mr. Brandon, how do I impress my girlfriend for Valentine's Day?"

It was tempting to pass on the practice-kissing-a-deer-head information but instead I said, "Well, you know, a small box of candy would be nice. I think she would like that."

"And maybe some flowers?" he added.

Before long I saw him working on something in his seat. He had taken some paper and rolled it up into a long object that looked something like a lightsaber. It looked pretty nice for a rolled-up piece of paper.

Well, he showed it to me and told me it looked kind of like a bunch of flowers, and he did this because he didn't have any real flowers. I assured him that it looked good and would be okay.

He got off the bus with it and the next day, he brought it back. On the ride home I asked him three or four times to quit hitting and poking people with it. By the time we reached his stop, it was pretty ragged-looking.

As he got off, he passed a young lady, handed it to her and said, "Here, happy Valentine's Day. Made it myself."

He kept walking.

I closed the door and looked in the mirror at a rather shocked little girl, who looked back and said, "What in the world is this?"

I hoped that if he did give her the box of candy it would not be half eaten.

A Little Off the Top

One morning a young man boarded the bus all smiles because he was sporting a new haircut.

"Man, that's a good-looking haircut," I greeted him.

"Thanks," he replied. "We went to Fayetteville Saturday."

Fayetteville happens to be one of those small Southern towns built around the old town square where many little shops surround the courthouse and things remain somewhat like they have been for many years.

I knew several barbers there, and get my hair cut there also, so I asked, "Did you get it cut on the Square?"

"No, sir, just round on the sides and a little off the top."

Halloween's Full Moon

One of the often-quoted lines from *The Godfather* is spoken by Peter Clemenza after the revenge killing of Paulie Gatto. Clemenza instructs Rocco Lampone, "Leave the gun, take the cannoli."

This advice was all about taking care of business and keeping one's priorities straight. We've all heard countless lectures and sermons to the same point. By taking care of the important task first and not letting ourselves get sidetracked by the trivial, we become productive and successful.

A kindergartener was struggling as he came up the aisle on the Friday before Halloween. One hand held onto his book bag that was bulging with the necessities of a day in kindergarten. The other hand held the haul of candy from the class party and the special treats that had been so lovingly made by his teacher.

Just wrangling these burdens had proved to be a daunting task, but as he prepared to leave the bus another problem made itself known. His pants were creeping down. Like most kindergarten boys, he didn't have much behind area to keep them up, and he was not wearing a belt.

He tried dragging his wrist across the waist of his pants, as if the pants might somehow stick to his wrist and he could pull them up. No go, so as he took the first step down, so did the pants. Another step, another slide of the pants. On the bottom step, he did a hula motion to try to impede the inevitable, but as his feet hit the ground, so did his pants.

There before me was the full Halloween moon. He was appropriately dressed with little orange pumpkins on his drawers.

He looked down at his fallen pants. He looked at his right hand, full of a book bag that he dared not put down. He looked at his left hand, full of a big bag of candy.

Then he showed that this was a young man with a bright future, his priorities firmly in place.

He hung onto what was important and waddled to the house with his pants around his ankles.

Intervention Needed

Hot Pickle Boy leaned in close and said quietly, "You know that little station over by the old store? Go in there and that Mexican guy named Jose, behind the counter, can get you what you want."

He slowly reached into his backpack. "That's where I got this. Here, take some and try it."

He handed me the beef stick.

Like any good supplier would, he gave me free beef sticks for two days and then cut me off.

By then the beef stick monkey was on my back and I knew that it was going to cost me.

I wondered if there was a place that specialized in beef stick rehab.

The Older Woman

When she stepped onto the bus for the first time it was like a new Ferrari driving onto a used car lot. All eyes were immediately focused on her.

A high school girl, on a bus filled with elementary school boys.

A hush fell over the bus because the boys had quit breathing. As she walked down the aisle to the back of the bus, little boy heads, with gap-toothed smiles and goofy haircuts, turned as if on swivels. As she passed, they inhaled her perfume, which they knew immediately was worlds better than the usual bus smells.

Even a six-year-old can tell when an older woman has got it all going on.

As the bus lurched forward, their dreamy, wide-eyed gazes gradually returned to the front of the bus. The silence was broken by a rather excited first-grader with an astute observation: "Ohhhh, Mr. Brandon, girls sure are pretty."

Unable to disagree with such sound logic, I said, "They sure are."

"Mr. Brandon," he continued, "is it fun to kiss a girl?"

I looked at him in the mirror and said, "Not till you're eighteen, it's not."

A smile formed on his pale, pudgy, freckled face and he said, "I don't think I can wait that long."

A Pause Can Kill You

He stepped up and calmly said, "Mr. Brandon, I just touched my dangly, hangy down thing."

He paused; I quit breathing.

"With this finger."

Another pause; still not breathing.

"You know, that hangy down thing in the back of your throat."

Okay, breathe.

Friends to the Ends

As the kindergartener stood at the bus steps, I asked, "Did you have a good day?"

"Well, not too good. We had to go to the principal's office," she replied.

"To the office?"

"Well, me and my friend got in trouble in P.E. and had to go to the office."

The usual P.E. offenses ran through my mind: fighting, throwing something, not following directions. None of these things seemed likely from these little cherubs. She went on, "Well, she pulled down her pants and showed her hiney, so I decided I would, too."

Clearly I had not been expansive enough in my mental run-down of potential infractions. But hoping lessons had already been learned, I replied simply, "Well you know that's not something that good girls do, and I'm sure you just did it because you thought it would be funny."

"Yes, but it didn't turn out as funny as we thought it would," she said.

It is hard to talk about correcting bad behavior when you really want to crack up laughing.

Honk Honk

It has been pressed upon us that our children are the future. Therefore, we have been bombarded with the idea that we must care for the planet now, so there will be sufficient resources for our children to enjoy.

Politicians, television, and celebrities speak of the evils of our out-of-control consumption. All of this has led to the re-emergence of the smaller, fuel-efficient car. Down with the evil luxury vehicle.

We hope to have instilled in today's youth a different vision of the future.

As I rounded the corner to drop Mr. Mucus off at his house, there it was—a small, million-miles-to-the-gallon hybrid. A marvel of engineering that would make the greenest tree-hugger proud.

He looked at it in all its shining glory and said, "Hey, Mr. Brandon, there's a clown car in my yard. What's up with that?"

Oh, well. Maybe they can brainwash the next generation.

Random Thoughts—It Won't Kill You

When my grandfather said, "Boys, come with me down to the shop. I've got a job for you," we knew exactly what he meant.

He would reach into the corner of the shop, remove a hoe, place it in a vise on the workbench, and with a few quick file swipes it would have a nice, sharp edge.

He would hand the hoe to one of us and repeat the actions twice more till each of us stood with tool in hand.

We would then step out of the shop and he would point to some part of the farm and say, "You boys start over there and I want you to hoe out all the thistles, milkweeds, and cactus that you find."

The key word was start, there was no "When you reach there you can stop." There was a start but no stop. On a large farm in Oklahoma there were enough thistles, milkweeds, and cactus for a lifetime of employment. There were occasional stops for water, then back to the house for lunch, and the afternoon would find us in the shade of the pecan trees down by the creek. But for the most part it was hot, dusty, and sweaty. Not exactly what one looks forward to.

Most of us recall similar stories, with the effort and severity of the job growing with the passing of time. We delight in telling the younger how lucky they are and how hard we had it.

Yet we are here to tell the stories, so the work did not kill us nor drive us to hate our fellow man. As parents, we try to help our children by providing better for them than what we may have had as children ourselves. We try to keep them from what are sometimes perceived as hardships of everyday life. We don't want them to have to do without or work as hard as we felt that we had to, even if the severity is only self-perceived.

Most of all, we have memories because of those times that bring joy to our hearts; we would not trade them for anything in the world, though at the time we thought we would surely die.

I am afraid that as we try to remove perceived struggles that we also rob our children of experiences that would make them stronger and richer. Many would agree that some of our favorite memories that we share with our spouse are the times we were struggling together to make that first little house a home and crying and laughing when our children cried and laughed.

That which we hold the dearest is what we have poured ourselves into, both mentally and physically. The struggles that our children and grandchildren face in moving from level five to level six of their favorite video game will be forgotten, but the sweat and labor involved in earning that game will bring a feeling of satisfaction and make them stronger people.

Thanks to my parents and grandparents for the memories and, yes, hard work that I will always treasure. When I look back on those times, they make my life full.

Oh, if you were wondering about pay, from time to time because of our hard work our grandfather would take us to town to the local café. We would all sit at the counter and could have all the foot-long hotdogs we could eat.

Well, maybe it was not because of our hard work, but just because he was a grandfather. Because I know how that feels, too.

Patriotism: Pass It On

He stepped onto the bus in all of his patriotic glory. Smiling from ear-to-ear, he was proudly wearing a do-rag—you know, the cloths worn by bikers under their helmets.

His was red, white, and blue with stars. Before I had an opportunity to say anything, the Twins Who Are Not Twins stood, placed their hands over their hearts, and started, "I pledge allegiance to the Flag of the United States of America and to the Republic for which it stands, one Nation under God, indivisible, with liberty and justice for all."

They finished with, "Let us now have a moment of silence." Those who had been caught off guard by the pledge were able to join in the moment of silence.

The moment of silence did not last long enough, but at this point I had to hum "God Bless America."

A Rock Unmoved

An attribute that seems to be missing in our ever-changing society is perseverance—you know, staying with it when the odds seem against you, the road is rocky, and life wants to reach in and snatch away your joy.

Mr. Mucus boarded and said, "Mr. Brandon, look what I've got."

It was an old, beat-up camera. He explained that the neighbor had been cleaning out some junk and gave it to him. He asked if I had a photo battery and I told him no. Not to be deterred, he began taking pictures.

As a first-grade girl stepped on the bus, he threw up his camera and said, "Smile." She promptly stopped, smiled, and did that girl thing where they throw out a hip and put a hand on it. I guess it's in their DNA. She walked on, and he commented, "She's such a great smiler."

He continued to take pictures until he informed us that he had taken 193 pictures and was going to stop because he didn't want the batteries to run down. Mr. Bubble Buster said, "You don't even have any batteries in that camera."

Where others might have faltered, Mr. Mucus stood his ground: "Yes, but I don't want the imaginary batteries to run down, either."

Remember, stay true to what brings you joy, and be great at something, even if it's being a great smiler.

'Tis the Season

We were in the excessive heat of August. That is why, as I was taking home the last student on a rather long route and heard her humming and singing Christmas songs, I said, "Wow, are you trying to get Christmas to hurry up and get here?"

"No, Mr. Brandon," she said, "I've got to go to the bathroom real bad and I have to do something to take my mind off it."

Well, I tried to help by singing along, but she didn't appreciate it when I changed the words to, "Ooooh I haaaaave got to peeee."

She made it home and was humming a tune as she jumped from the bus. I laughed about it a little as I headed back, but by the time I reached school I was doing a little "Jingle Bell Rock" step myself.

Scouting

Excited about the homework he had finished, the second-grader was showing off his "All About Me" poster to the other kids. He was pointing out the pictures and talking about how hard he had worked on it, when a fourth-grader pointed out a problem.

"I think you used the wrong letter on that word."

The argument went back and forth, but the fourth-grader had reason on his side when he said, "I'm pretty sure you did not mean to say that you are in the 'Doy' Scouts."

The second-grader was understandably upset.

He said if he got a low grade then his dad might not take him on vacation to "Hoowhyyee." Between Doy Scouts and the great state of Hoowhyyee, I think you know I was not dropping anyone off at the Academy for Advanced Placement.

Security

When you're young there is oh so much time to plan for the future. You know . . . retirement. Then the years pass and you get closer and closer to what seemed an age away. Then worries come to mind. Will I have enough to get by? What will I do? It can cause considerable distress and worry.

Yet my mind is at ease, with no worry, no sleepless nights. My future is bright. Yes, bright, thanks to that trustworthy, loyal, helpful, friendly, courteous, kind, obedient, cheerful, thrifty, brave, clean, and reverent Boy Scout, Mr. Mucus.

He informed me that he was selling popcorn for the Boy Scouts, and that he was going to make $356 million. When he had made that fortune, he was going to let me drive him around in his limousine. The perks would not stop there. I would be allowed to be a part of Den 223, though I would have to buy a Boy Scout shirt from the Boy Scout Store.

Mr. Mucus had more than lived up to the Boy Scout slogan, "Do a good turn daily!" He had given hope to a weary soul.

Do not envy me. That was not my intent. For one day I may give you a ride in the limo.

Signs Along the Old Bus Trail

I believe if most successful bus drivers were to trace their ancestry, they would find they are descendants of the trackers seen in the old westerns. They can look at the ground and can tell how many horses came this way, and how one was carrying a one-legged man with a patch over his left eye. They can put their hands in the coals of an old campfire and tell you how long the fugitives have been gone and what they ate for supper.

Bus drivers become similarly expert at spotting signs and reading their meanings along the old bus trail.

- Student pauses and looks at you with extra-large smile: You are to notice missing teeth.
- Little girl swishes hair when crossing the road: You are to comment on new haircut.
- Student pauses and looks down at feet: Compliment new shoes.
- Student looks at you with eyes wider than normal: New glasses.
- Student looks down at feet, one foot forward: Needs help tying shoe.
- Boy that usually runs to the bus walks extremely slowly to bus: Sister not ready; mom has told him to stall for time.
- Last student off the bus in the morning stops, looks at you, and grins: They need a hug before they go to class and they didn't want anyone else to know. (Little boys often also need you to pretend to punch them in the stomach or act like you're putting knots on their head.)

Eveready

During the winter months, the sun is slow to slip over the horizon, so the first few pick-ups are often in the dark. Who else would come to our rescue but the ever faithful, always vigilant, Mr. Mucus.

As he boarded one morning, he was digging in his book bag as he announced, "Don't worry, I'm a Scout. I'm always prepared—look what I've got, Mr. Brandon."

I looked as he clicked on a flashlight whose original packaging must have said: "Own a piece of the sun."

While the flash burns to my retinas were healing, he pointed out the great help he could be. "I can help you see the road," as he pointed it out the front window.

"I can look for lost things under the seats," and all I could see was his bottom sticking up in the air as he took a dive.

"And we can keep an eye on them," he continued, pointing the light at two little girls who had been known to be up to no good.

Like many bright ideas, this one's time came and went quickly. Within a few minutes, the sun had eased up, overpowering even Mr. Mucus's spotlight. But, putting aside those students who were recovering from a bout of temporary blindness, it wasn't that bad of an idea.

Pendulum Swing

With all the crazy conversations that go on, it is refreshing to have a true scientific conversation with a student. One day a fourth-grader was in the mood to talk and wanted to discuss space.

We talked of stars, planets, galaxies, the speed of light, and the possibility of space exploration and colonization. We talked of the unfathomable wonders of the universe.

Also mentioned was that since the morning was so foggy, it reminded him of the zombie apocalypse and he needed to practice patting his head and rubbing his belly. Apparently this will protect you from a zombie attack.

Just one of the interesting facts of the universe.

Perspective

A small inquisitive voice asked, "Mr. Brandon, what are those things for?"

I glanced over my left shoulder to see the eyes and nose of a young man struggling to see over the partition between us. "What things do you mean?" I asked.

"All those buttons and knobs by you," he said, indicating the switches next to me.

So I told him how they worked the heaters, air conditioners, and other devices on the bus. The feature that outdid them all was the lever that moved the steering wheel up and down. He got off the bus in a state of wonder. The next day he was behind me again, but now he was the teacher, passing on the knowledge he had gained the day before.

He explained to a fascinated little girl what each of the switches did. He saved the best till last and said, "Mr. Brandon, show her what that lever does."

So I pulled on it and raised the wheel up and then lowered it back down. Then he finished his instructional talk with, "Isn't my bus wonderful?"

Make your day better and go through it with the wonder and fascination of a four-year-old. Look with wonder at the switches to flick, knobs to turn, and levers to pull.

Ask how birds find their way home, why cats purr and babies coo, how the touch of someone's hand can make you feel warm inside, and how a child's kiss on your cheek can almost make you cry.

Don't overlook the wonder of the smallest detail. Take nothing for granted.

Then say, "Isn't my world wonderful."

Herculean Task

The kindergarteners struggled toward the bus in a single-file line, bent over, and staggering under their loads like the children of Israel in Egypt. Their backpacks were bulging to the point of exploding.

It could only mean one thing, which was confirmed by a thud followed by a large orange sphere rolling down the aisle.

Yes, the kindergarteners had made their annual trip to the pumpkin patch. Each backpack now contained a pumpkin that appeared to outdo its owner in size and weight.

There have been studies on how much weight an insect can carry compared to body size. I believe an ant cannot compete with the field-trip adrenaline rush of an excited five-year-old when he is selecting a pumpkin to carry home.

Miscommunication

Most schools have a week during the year when they celebrate a special event by letting the students do something each day that they would not normally do.

Maybe the students all wear their favorite hat one day. Or they might have a day when everybody wears camouflage (of course, in our small rural farming and hunting community, that would not be so special, since camouflage is what your parents probably were wearing on their first date).

On one particular day, our students were allowed to wear tie-dyed clothing. Which explains why a second-grader hopped up the steps of the bus, smiling from ear to ear, with one of his father's ties around his neck.

"Mr. Brandon," he said, "it's tie dye day."

Not to rain on his parade, I told him it looked great and he went happily on down the aisle.

A much wiser fourth-grader looked at me in my mirror and said, "But it's tie-dye day! Tie DYE day!" I looked back at him and slowly shook my head no.

He looked at the second-grader, who was now proudly showing the tie to other students. "Just leave it alone?" he mouthed to me. I replied with an affirmative nod.

Math Word Problem

Bus Driver B drives a standard school bus rated at 72 passengers with 24 seats. Keep in mind these seats were designed for occupancy by three elves, not one average Oreo-eating, chocolate-cake-loving, normal modern kid.

Driver B transports 65 students consisting of: 13

groups of siblings who cannot sit next to each other because of hitting and fussing; 2 groups of neighborhood children who cannot sit next to each other because they can't get along in the neighborhood; 1 group of neighborhood children who can't sit by each other because their parents can't get along; 2 kindergarteners who can't sit by the windows because they lick the glass; 12 assorted 4-5-year-olds who believe a bus is a wonderland to be explored because it's the first vehicle they have ever ridden in without being strapped down in some way; and the children of 8 mothers who each want their child to sit in the front seat so you can keep an eye on them.

Question: Where should each child sit, and, more importantly, how many days will it be before Driver B needs a substitute so he can take a day off for mental health reasons?

Don't Forget to Twirl

As we near the end of the workday or school day, we think of the things that we're going to do when we get home. Sometimes, much to our dismay, things happen to deter our plans.

One afternoon on the route home, a chorus of moans erupted from the riders, for it had started to rain.

Afternoon plans were a bust and the dreariness set in.

I pulled up to the next drive, ready to open the door to a gray afternoon for another child.

The kindergarten girl looked at me and said with a smile, "I love the rain."

She hopped off the bus, took a few steps, twirled herself around a couple of times, then hurried on her way.

It made my day so much better; I smile every time I think about it.

Give yourself a twirl, even if you have to wait until no one is looking. Personally, I think if you twirl *while* they are looking, it will give you and them something to smile about.

It's in the Smile

Here's the difference between poorly behaved bus riders and well-behaved riders:

The poorly behaved riders give you the evil eye and grumble under their breath each of the twelve times you have to tell them to sit down during a ten-minute period.

The well-behaved riders smile sweetly and say, "Yes sir," each of the twelve times you tell them to sit down.

Top Ten Southern Advantages

The advantages of driving a bus in the rural South:

10. You don't have to drive on snow. Schools are dismissed if a single snowflake is spotted in the next county.

9. A cotton field can make a picturesque turnaround spot.

8. You get samples of homemade jerky from your riders.

7. Shopping in Walmart on Friday night allows you to speak to any parents you need to talk to.

6. Wild turkeys crossing the road can give you some time for peaceful reflection.

5. The only arguments about fashion are over which camo pattern is better.

4. No matter how many students you have on your bus, it can all be narrowed down to one or two families.

3. Students can give advice on how to get rid of varmints, four-legged or two.

2. You get to talk about hunting with a third-grader who shows you a picture of the buck she shot that morning, while she was standing on her back porch.

1. You can yell, "Bubba, stop that!" and half the students on the bus will stop what they're doing.

Please Let It Be a Weapon

Often families use words differently than how they are defined in the dictionary. I received a shocked look from a young man once when I called him a little goober—meaning, I intended, a peanut. Then the mom informed me how they use the word goober at home.

Sorry.

So when a young man boarded the bus, reached for his sweat pants and said, "Let me show you my nunchakus," it was the only time I have ever thought, "Please, let him be reaching for a martial arts weapon."

Much to my relief, he pulled out a set of nunchakus. Okay, one problem avoided.

Next, why was an energized second-grader bringing nunchakus to school? It seems he had done well on his progress report and Dad had bought him a gift.

Good move Dad!

I'm not a prophet, but I asked to keep up with the nunchakus on the way to school, just to avoid the "Mr. Brandon, he just hit me" dramas.

Let's hope the young man doesn't make straight A's on his next report card.

Champion

As a second-grader came to the bus, I could tell he was wearing something on his right hand.

I knew what it looked like but there was a small part of me that was sure I was wrong. He came up the steps, held up his right hand and said, "Guess what, Mr. Brandon?"

Sure enough, it was as I had thought, a surgical glove with the ends of the fingers cut out. He snapped the glove against his wrist and said, "Do you know what I am?"

I took another look at the upheld gloved hand with the missing finger ends, and I wanted to say, "A really careless proctologist?"

But using better judgment, I simply said, "I don't know."

"I'm a champion bowler," he said, "and have been for the past four years."

As he demonstrated his bowling form, I breathed a sigh of relief.

Perpetrator

The young lady's rather distraught look got my attention even before she said, "Mr. Brandon, that boy back there has a real Okie Pokie."

Then she went and sat down.

I wasn't sure how to react to a real Okie Pokie. I mean, I understood Okie Dokie and even Hokie Pokie.

But Okie Pokie was a new one. I thought, maybe it's a version of the dance only done in Oklahoma.

Trying not to panic at the prospect of a rider with a real Okie Pokie on board, I watched where she sat to see who around her might be the perpetrator.

And there he was.

Mr. Mucus and I realized immediately what she was talking about. When he got on the bus that morning he showed me what he had brought. It was a walkie-talkie.

Mystery solved, he had even been trying to talk to his friend because he was saying, "Breaker, breaker." When I asked what his friend's name was, he gave me a look like "really," then he said, "Breaker."

I should have known.

Kid Bell

He held up two cups that were attached together with a long piece of string. With the pride of any true inventor, he told me what it was.

He really didn't have to; I know a well-crafted phone when I see one.

Then he demonstrated how it worked. One rider held

a cup up to my ear as the other one stood behind me and yelled into the other cup, "Mr. Brandon, Mr. Brandon."

The clarity was amazing! It was almost like he was right behind me yelling my name.

Next, they moved on to a test of long distance. I heard one say, "Ciao" and the other one said, "Sayonara."

I hope they have the right phone plan, because those international charges can be outrageous.

Your Order, Please

A second-grader boarded the bus with a small cloth pocketed apron of the type that carpenters keep nails in while they work.

Before he was seated he asked if I would help him tie it on. I pulled the bow tight in the back, expecting a "Bob the Builder" moment. But he turned to face me, pulled out a piece of paper and a pen and asked, "Can I take your order, sir?"

I asked him to be seated, but, being a little hungry, gave him my order: "Two eggs over easy, hash browns, biscuits and gravy, and country ham."

He read it back to me, had the eggs wrong but corrected it, then turned to a fourth-grader seated across from him and yelled, "Order up!" and handed him the paper.

The fourth-grader looked at me a little confused, shrugged his shoulders, waited a few seconds, and yelled back, "Okay, pick up."

I must admit, the service was fast and friendly.

By this time, he was taking the orders of the two young ladies behind him. One ordered a sausage biscuit and the other said she was on a diet and wanted a blueberry muffin.

Over all, it was a good dining experience. I would give it three and a half stars.

My only complaint was that he told me about the special they were having on oatmeal after he had already turned in my order.

But it probably wouldn't have mattered, as he wasn't sure the kitchen had any oatmeal left because a man last night had ordered one thousand bowls and a piece of sausage.

Tour Bus

There was a loud "ONE," followed by a click, then "TWO," click.

From the voice I knew exactly where to look. Looking in the mirror I spied the snowman-shaped second-grader with his little round face and round body. His face was as red as his hair, and he held a pencil in each hand over his head.

"THREE," click. On "FOUR," click, his hands with the magic pencils came down on the seatback in front of him and began a drum solo that would have made any rock drummer envious.

Then he yelled out, "Gentlemen, I believe we have found ourselves a DRUMMER!"

I held my breath waiting for the finale that all great drummers are known for, and I was not disappointed. The energy and beat crescendoed, he threw up his hands, a pencil sailed to the back of the bus, and—hands still upraised—he screamed out, "WE LOVE YOU WORLD PEACE!"

A wipe of the forehead and all was quiet.

In my mind's eye, I already see his smiling face on the cover of *Rolling Stone*. I'm going to get five copies for my . . .

Go ahead and sing it.

I did.

Freedom

A kindergartener stepped up beside me. His eyes were as wide as they could be and still be contained in their sockets. His mouth hung open and he was point-ing to his right.

I asked what he wanted, but he remained very ex-cited, did not speak a word, and continued motioning to his right.

So, I looked to his right. There, seated very quietly, were three little girls. You could not ask for three little girls to sit any more still or quiet than they were.

Yet there was something not quite right with the picture. The little girl in the middle, though a model of perfect posture, was topless.

To be fair, all of her older siblings are boys who run around the neighborhood without their shirts. Taking into account the double standard, I quietly said, "You need to put your shirt back on."

With a big smile on her face she replied, "But it's hot on the bus."

I shook my head in agreement and continued, "I know, but we need to put our shirt back on."

She countered with, "You know it takes longer to put a shirt on than it does to take one off."

Following that line of thought, I encouraged her to see how fast she could put a shirt on. She obliged and we continued on down the road without incident.

All was well, except for the poor kindergarten boy who

may have to see an optometrist. When I let him off the bus, a wide-eyed expression was still frozen to his face.

Random Thoughts—Listen

Walk into any rural, small-town cafe or restaurant and you'll find it in the front or back corner. It can be rectangular or round, but regardless of its shape or location it often is referred to by the same name: "The Liars' Table."

Seated around it you will find a variety of men, for the most part older men who are retired, close to retiring, or those who will never retire regardless of their age.

They share jokes with one another. Often the joke has been told a number of times due to the fact that the teller has forgotten that he told it on a previous occasion. Most of the time that's okay, because the listeners don't remember hearing it, and those who do laugh like it was the first time.

Sometimes you will find a jar of homemade jelly that has been provided by one of the regulars. As the men come and go, for they are never all there at the same time, they talk and share stories. Some of the stories, as you can imagine, should not be repeated in polite company.

As they tell their stories they reveal the paths that they have walked. Though their backgrounds are varied they have two common threads: laughter and hard work. To many, it would seem these two things do not go together. Surely joy and laughter can only be found in avoiding hard work. Yet if you listen carefully, the hard work in their lives has let them enjoy the little things along the way all that much more.

They know what it is to rise before the sun and come home after sunset. They have come home covered from head to toe with dirt and smelling of sweat, collapse in exhaustion, then rise and start all over. Many of those jobs offered no pay; they were for friends and relatives, and they were raised in a generation where relationships were more important than pay.

Now they look back and find humor in those times of stress and worry. As they tell their often-exaggerated stories you also realize they are the community historians, because they talk of "remember when." They often argue about dates but they remember the big snow, the flood, the tornado that devastated the community, and where you could go to buy local moonshine. They remember when the Smith farm was the Johnson farm and before that it was the Jones farm, or how an old man that everybody called Uncle John would always give you a ride in his wagon if you needed it.

They give direction not only by road names but by

landmarks like that big old oak tree, that old two-story house they tore down, Steger's curve, or over on the creek at Hump.

They are the history of the community, for they have grown up here, worked here, and buried loved ones in the family plots in the local cemeteries.

As our society continues to change, what will become of the liars' table? We have become so mobile that few live where they were born and even fewer know the bone-tiring labor that was commonplace for another generation.

Not many contemporary relationships go back more than a few years. We don't know who lives next door, much less the history of that old house down on the corner. I often wonder what will happen when no one remembers where the best pear tree in the county is, or what will happen when we lose men of character who would not increase the size of their field because it would mean cutting down that pear tree.

These men are not only found around this table. They are at our own table during family get-togethers and holidays, they are sitting on the pew next to us at church, they are on the porch of the house across the street.

Take time to listen, because one day, where there was history and character, there will be silence.

Uninvited

A young man was talking about a trip he was going to take over the weekend. He mentioned where he would stay and most importantly where he would eat.

You could tell he was very excited.

The conversation was directed to those around him, especially his on-again, off-again girlfriend sitting behind him. She spoke up and said, "It doesn't sound like a very fun trip to me."

Putting his hands on his hips he replied, "Well, I'll have you to know that this trip is important to me and you should be happy for me."

The conversation escalated in volume so I stepped in with, "Both of you need to be happy and stop fussing."

"We are happy," he replied. "This is what is called a RELATIONSHIP." He paused for a few seconds and said, "I don't think you'll be invited to the wedding."

Though I was heartbroken, I tried to control my emotions and asked, "Why?"

He said, "Do you really want to see us kiss?"

You cannot argue with sound logic. Count me as not invited.

Weather Aware

On a rather cloudy day a second-grader entered the bus. After the usual morning pleasantries he moved to his seat.

Before he sat down he opened his book bag and pulled something out. In a few moments he was sitting as any student should with one exception: he was now wearing a skateboard helmet.

So I asked, "Hey, what's that all about?"

"Well, I read that in a tornado a skateboard helmet can protect your head and I just wanted to be ready," he replied.

Then there was a quiet discussion between him and the other students around him. I was sure it was about his diligence in making others aware of the possibilities for weather safety.

Then with a puzzled look on his face he asked, "Mr. Brandon, what's a nit-wit?"

My reply was, "Most of the people on this bus."

Genetic

As we were going down the road, she stepped out into the aisle with a wide smile on her face and started making her way to the front with a bouncy little step.

I saw she was wearing a Batman shirt that she has a fondness for. Knowing how unsafe it was for her to be walking down the aisle of a moving bus, I said, "Batman, you need to sit down."

I know, I referred to her as Batman, but I had called Batgirl in the past and was quickly put straight on the matter, lesson learned.

I tried again with a little more parental tone in my voice: "Batman, you need to sit down."

She was not deterred but the smile had now turned to a frown. So I pulled out all stops and referred to her by her real name and said, "You need to sit down."

Now not only was the smile gone, but her little head hung down. At this point she was by my side. Knowing I had lost the battle, I asked, "What do you need?"

She raised her head, looked at me with those big dark eyes and said, "But, I just wanted to tell you that I love you, Mr. Brandon."

I replied, "I love you, too, baby, but you need to stay sitting down."

With a look that was far from happy or understanding she made her way back to her seat.

Women! How do they do that? I truly believe it is genetic. They can all do it.

She had executed it perfectly.

1. She had gotten her way no matter the obstacles.

2. Though I knew with every fiber in my body I was right and every safety manual ever written would say that I was right, I, yes, now felt like a heel.

3. She would be over it in just a few minutes and I would feel bad about being right the rest of the day.

There is not a man born who hasn't been the recipient of cunning female behavior.

Multitasking

Pride is a tricky thing.

We encourage our children to take pride in their work and then we warn of the downfall of being too prideful. We brag on our kids and tell them how proud we are of them and then point out those that are too full of themselves.

It is a slippery slope. Yet there are moments when you know you have achieved something that is at the pinnacle of its type.

I don't think Michelangelo, after he finished the statue of David, said, "Oh, just slide it over in the corner someplace." And I'm pretty sure that when he finished the Sistine Chapel ceiling he said the Italian equivalent of, "Get on some of that!"

So I was not at all surprised when a fourth-grade boy proudly told me of an accomplishment guaranteed to bring pride and respect to the rank and file of young men everywhere.

With a gleam in his eyes and pride in his voice, he said, "Mr. Brandon, I just burped, farted, and sneezed all at the same time."

Go West, Young Man

The young student stepped onto the bus with the confidence and resolve of a modern-day Meriwether Lewis.

He was dressed in cargo shorts with the standard 150 pockets filled with the items needed for a grueling trek across the vast wilderness. His T-shirt extended well below his waistline and he wore a black dress belt *over* the T-shirt. On the belt was a small nylon pouch.

He stepped beside me and, with the sound of Velcro being parted, produced a compass from the small pouch. He held it out for me to see and informed me, "I will be keeping us on track today."

He looked at the compass with a concentration only known by those who realize that the lives and safety of innocent people are in their hands.

He pointed down the road and said, "That direction

is—" There was a momentary pause as he found his bearings. "That direction is . . . thataway." He shrugged his shoulders and said, "Hey, I looked at the directions and they looked hard, so I'm not exactly sure how this thing works yet."

Lucky for us the school was due thataway from where we were.

Parental Neglect

Sooner or later young boys start to ask questions.

Many parents neglect to talk to their children about facts they should know. Often they leave that up to teachers or hope their children will learn it from their older siblings or maybe from their friends.

I don't know if it's the awkwardness of the questions or the fear that they may introduce information to their child before they are really old enough to understand.

On the route one day, a curious young man approached me with some questions. It may not have been my place, but I thought I would answer him as honestly as I could.

While I tried to explain the whole parental dynamic, another young man across the aisle tossed in some half-truths showing that he, too, did not understand the facts.

After I finished, the boy's face took on an ashen color, and there was a drawn out "Whaaaaat?"

I think we can all relate. There is not one of us that did not have the same reaction when we found out that Darth Vader was Luke Skywalker's dad.

Then I think I lost him when I tried to explain that movies 4, 5, and 6 came before 1, 2, and 3. I think he will figure it all out in time.

Parents, make sure your kids know the facts and don't pick up misinformation on the street. It's not safe.

Apologies

I did not really want to put him off the bus.

He had treated me kinder than anyone else that day. There was no doubt in my mind that he was the smartest one on the bus. Everyone on the bus seemed to like him. But his behavior was just not acceptable.

From the time he stepped on the bus, he was down the aisle, back up the aisle, and down again. He seemed oblivious to what I was trying to tell him. He had the whole bus in an uproar.

It was clear that I would have to set the parking brake, turn on the flashing lights, and get up out of my seat if I was going to get control of the situation. Traffic on the road was now backing up in both directions.

I tried to talk to him in a calm manner, with no effect. So I had no other choice but to go down the aisle and confront him.

Just as I was in reach, he crawled under a seat. There was no way out except back to me. He didn't move, so I asked the students in the seat to lift their legs so he could exit out the front of the seat. He came out and with me behind him, he had no choice but to move toward the front. I directed him right to the front and off the bus, closing the door as quickly behind him as I could. He turned and gave me a quick look that would have broken a lesser man's will.

But I knew it was a lesson he had to learn. I released the parking brake and drove on. I could see in the rear view mirror that he took a few steps toward the bus as we drove off and then gave up.

To all who were stuck in the traffic jam while I dealt with this problem, I apologize.

And if that dog—the size of a small pony—gets on my bus again, I'm bringing him to school. I feel that in dog years he should be a high school student, so I will let him transfer over to the high school bus and go on from there.

Gift Advice

It all started the day before when the Twins That Are Not Twins asked if I had gotten my wife a present.

Being a man, I was not sure if I had forgotten some national holiday or if I had forgotten a personal day and my wife had made some calls to put the word out. I informed them that I had not gotten my wife a present.

Immediately I was verbally attacked in stereo with, "How come?" and "Why not?"

Being females, they followed the criticism with gifting advice. "Mr. Brandon, it's not that hard. If you can't buy anything just go into her room and find a ring or necklace that she is not wearing, put it in a box or bag, and give it to her as a present."

They said they did that to their mom all the time and it worked just fine. The next day they felt they needed to follow up on our conversation and asked again, "Did you get your wife a present?" Again I had to answer, "No."

So they started in, "Mr. Brandon, just find any little thing with a hole in it, run a string through it, and you have a necklace. Come on, big man. You need to do something."

When I get a chance, I'm checking my wife's phone history to see who she has been calling.

Out of Context

As anyone who has ever worked in a school setting can tell you, school employees do not exist outside the boundaries of the school. When you meet one of your students in the grocery store or in a restaurant or Walmart—the motherland for most of your students—they look at you with little puzzled faces, trying to make the connection.

Well, at the start of the school year, bus drivers will make a trip around their route to check who has moved out, who has moved in, and who has rearranged their cars and basketball goals in the road to test your driving ability.

As I was making my rounds in my truck, I pulled into a drive where I turn around each morning of the school year. There sitting on the porch was my best buddy, Mr. Mucus, drinking a Coke.

I rolled down my window and yelled, "Hey, bring me a drink of that." He looked for a few seconds then ran out to talk to me. After an exchange of "How was your summer?" we came to the question that was perplexing his young mind: "Mr. Brandon, how did you know where I live?"

I paused for a moment, hoping that the answer would come to him ... no luck. "Could it be that I've been picking you up and driving you home from school each day for four years?"

The eyebrows went down and the look of deep thought came over him. He was not going to be tricked into giving a wrong answer. Then slowly a grin appeared on his face and he said, "Oh!"

Another mystery solved.

Adopted

One fine morning a first-grade girl who usually got on the bus full of excitement sat down behind me with a deep sigh. There was a pause, then a small soft voice said, "You know, Mr. Brandon, my papa died."

This is always difficult, because you never know what their understanding is of the situation. But I told her how sorry I was.

"Mr. Brandon," she said, "now that I don't have a papa, I'm going to need another one. I've been thinking, and I think it could be you."

How do you turn down an offer like that? I had never been adopted before. After that she would tell the kids at school that I was her papa. When they asked if I was, I always said yes.

Later there was a change of schools. Several years

passed and we lost contact with each other. Then my bus route changed and one day I stopped to pick up a group of older students, and guess who got on the bus?

A beautiful young lady whom I had known as a funny, full-of-life little girl.

I thought, do I say something and take the chance of looking like a foolish old man? You know, papas are like that sometimes. But I concluded, oh well, why not, and said, "How has my granddaughter been?"

She smiled and gave me a hug and said, "Just fine." As she got off the bus she said, "Goodbye, Papa."

It felt as good as the first time she said it.

Family. It either makes you crazy or it makes you smile. There's not much middle ground.

Escape

"Hey, Mr. Brandon, I'm going to tie myself up."

The cry had came from about two seats back and was from a young man who had always been quite "mobile," let us say.

So it sounded like a good idea to me. I had often thought of it myself, but the school system is a little picky about tying up students on the bus. I know—political correctness, run amuck.

He went to work with a long string that he had brought from home and seemed to be successful. Yet, it was not long and he was moving about again.

I gave him that "What are you doing?" look.

"Well, sorry," he said. "I did a Houdini on you."

Next time, I may supply chains and locks and see how that works out.

First Responder

The ear-piercing scream came as I stood at the bus door.

It was the kind of scream that causes the hair to stand up on the back of your neck, causes people of weak fiber to crumble and even the hearty to hesitate before charging into the fray.

Finding the strength that comes with a surge of adrenaline triggered by urgency, I turned and made a quick assessment of materials needed for what must be a near-death injury.

There was the first aid kit and the body-fluids-cleanup kit for the blood I was sure must be flowing freely. And I had not left campus yet, so I had access to the school nurse if necessary.

I stepped resolutely toward the sound that now was

a wailing befitting an Irish dirge. I looked into her little round face, and tears of a size I had never seen before were rolling down her cheeks at a rate that had left her whole face wet.

I looked for the missing limb that I was sure had been severed in some horrific accident. I could find neither blood nor wound. I knew then it must be internal and it must be excruciating because the wailing had now turned to sobs that made it difficult for her to breathe.

I tried to stay calm, knowing if I showed worry it might lead her to think the worst.

I took a deep breath and asked, "What's the matter?"

I knew it had to be bad, because it took a little time for her get to a state that she could communicate with me.

Finally she was able to say between sobs, "I . . . I . . . left my library book in the room."

In my kindest, most understanding voice, I could only reply, "Knock it off already."

Run, It's a Trap

Mother and child approached the large yellow symbol of education that had stopped in front of their house.

His excited, unsuspecting little smile was visible even from a distance. He knew this had to be a great adventure for she had led him on so many. His whole world stood beside him and she held his hand.

His new lunch box was swinging in his free hand and they were walking at a good pace. As they neared the large, unfamiliar conveyance, the doors swung open as if the mouth to a giant yellow creature that is only found in the dreams of little innocent children.

By now his stride had decreased and his smile had diminished. Mother and disillusioned child stopped at the cavernous mouth of the yellow monster. An unfamiliar voice came from its depths: "Good morning."

His mother had always told him to stay away from strangers and not to talk to people he didn't know, yet here she was offering him up without any regard for his personal feelings on the matter. He acted instinctively and slid behind his mother's legs. She pulled him back around in front only to have him retreat once more. Mother pulled him around again and nudged him forward. His feet remained firmly planted as if glued to the pavement.

Feeling himself being lifted, he went limp and Mother now struggled with the dead weight of an unwilling child. Then with the strength of a woman who had not had one day alone since his birth, a woman envisioning what an uninterrupted visit to the bathroom would be like, she lifted him to the first step.

He would not willingly go into the beast so she lifted him to the next step. There was still no action on his part; he would resist to the end.

From inside the bus, the voice, accented with a smile, encouraged the mother, "One more and I'll take care of the rest."

Spurred on by visions of a lunch that did not involve chicken nuggets or peanut butter, Mother stepped into the jaws of the yellow monster herself. She placed him on the top step and quickly moved back, her arm barely out of the way when the jaws of the yellow beast closed.

He turned, looked at his retreating mother and with a feeble hand reached out, but it was too late. He bravely turned to face the man he had never seen before. Without a tear or tremor he stood waiting.

The man pointed to an empty seat.

He gave in to what must be and was seated. Education would have its way.

Early the next morning, the yellow monster again pulled in front of his house. This time his steps were fast and he rushed willingly, with a smile on his face, into the beast's open mouth. Someone had done their job and had convinced this child that school was actually fun.

And that would change his whole world.

A Boy from the Past

He paused to look in the mirror before he went to sit down. He pulled out a comb and started working on a style of haircut I had not seen on a young boy for a long time.

He said, "Mr. Brandon, you really need to train your hair if you wear a flattop."

He continued to comb slowly with an upward motion. He put each hair in place in a way that would make a child of the fifties proud.

I asked if he could continue his hair training in his seat.

The next young man to get on sat next to him. This one's hair was all spiked up in the middle. They looked at each other and almost at the same time said, "Don't touch the hair."

Then they compared hairstyles and hair products. One said, "Flattop and Brylcreem, smells good." The other said, "Spike and Hair Gel, no smell."

I'll let you guess which one lives with his grandfather.

Guess Who?

If it is true that necessity is the mother of invention, then profit must be the father.

Even at the precious, innocent age of six and seven,

a group of boys were scheming—well, planning—ways to make money. They discussed and rejected a number of plans before settling on one they felt showed some promise: arrowheads.

If they could just find enough Indian arrowheads, they could sell them and make a lot of money. Places that they might find such items were talked over, and then one of them was hit by a wave of genius. "No, no, wait," he said. "Forget that. I've got it!"

There was a short pause, with all attention on him. The lack-of-money problem was about to be forever solved.

"A time machine. All we have to do is make a time machine and we'll be rich! . . . The only problem is I don't think I have all the parts we will need at my house."

The momentary monkey wrench in the gears was removed when another spoke up, "But I do at my house."

I was not sure if I should or should not pull for their success. I did know that these boys were a handful in the present. If they started popping in and out of my past, or worse, my future, I was going to need a break.

Silver Bracelets

I know that young children can get their feelings hurt easily, especially when it comes to things they hold dear.

But even I was surprised with the flow of tears from a kindergartener when I told her she could not have her handcuffs back until she got home.

Finding Rest

We have all been tired and in need of rest for our weary bodies. We have also known the weariness of spirit. A spirit in need of rejuvenation and rest cannot necessarily find comfort in a rested body, but a tired body can be strengthened by a renewed spirit.

I assume a student was weary in spirit when he leaned forward and said in a very soft subdued voice, "Mr. Brandon, do you think you could sing 'Amazing Grace' for me?"

After a few verses he said, "That was pretty good. That's my grandma's favorite song."

This must have put another rider to thinking, because in the same soft tones she asked, "Mr. Brandon, do you think you could—"she paused while I wondered what comfort her little spirit needed—"could you whistle the tune from the 'Andy Griffith Show'?"

We each find solace in our own way.

Family Tree

Students often bring along extra riders in the form of baby dolls, toy soldiers, and assorted stuffed animals. So it was not unusual when a kindergartener introduced me to his stuffed rabbit and said his name was Barnacle.

I was a little surprised when he said it was his son, but not as surprised as the fifth-grade girl he pointed at across the aisle and said, "She's the mother."

Mr. Grammar

Simile: a phrase that uses the word *like* or *as* to describe someone or something by comparing it with someone or something else that is similar.

Hearing a high-pitched squeal from the back half of the bus, I used my extensive knowledge of the English language and chose the only simile that would be appropriate for the situation.

With my bus-driver authoritative voice, I yelled, "Hey, whoever is doing that, stop squealing like a little girl!" Then I settled back in the glow of a job well done.

Immediately a little blonde head popped up and said, "But I am a little girl." The squealing continued, and I hummed softly to myself as we continued down the road.

Well played, little girl. Well played.

Pay It Forward

The elementary school equivalent of the Hollywood red-carpet treatment is picture day. Four steps up onto the bus, pause, pose in front of the driver, wait for the approving "Oh, wow, nice," or a thumbs-up signal.

A third-grader boarded, feeling good towards all mankind, and said, "When Dad helped me with my shirt this morning he said, 'Boy, you been losing some weight. You're looking good.'"

Nothing makes you kindly towards others like feeling good about yourself. So he passed on the good vibes. As a much older girl, a sixth-grader, got on the bus, he said with a slow, Barry White voice, for a third-grader, "Who's the pretty lady? You're looking sexy."

There was a time-out from the bus driver, explaining how the term "sexy" was inappropriate from a third-grader to a sixth-grader. After an understanding "Yes," he continued when a young man got on the bus with, "Looking good." The next young man received a "Looking sharp, keep that up and you'll have a girlfriend in no time at all."

After a few more comments to his fellow students he turned his remarks to me. He said, "You know, Mr. Brandon, when it comes to picture day"—I prepared myself for the compliment to come—"you might want to lose a little weight for next year's pictures. Lay off the hamburgers."

I'm now rethinking my choices for lunch ... and whether he is walking home this afternoon.

Bold Move

She sat down behind me on the bus next to a young man who was in her class. There was the usual conversation that goes on between a boy and girl in elementary school.

Then I overheard this from him: "You are the most beautiful girl that I know and I think I love you."

"Whoa, big boy!" I said. "Slow down. Slow down."

"That's what I'm trying to tell him," she replied.

"Hey, Mr. Brandon," he said, "be quiet, I'm trying to get a date here."

I'm not sure where the conversation went after that. It must have gone well because as they got off the bus she was wearing his camouflage hat.

And we all know what sharing a hat at the elementary school level means. That's right, they will both have head lice before the week is out.

They say love is blind, but it can also be itchy.

Deep in the Heart of . . .

Most of you understand that I have many nicknames for the students that ride the bus each day. Some of the nicknames I actually call them when they are on the bus and some I only use here to protect the innocent or guilty.

As the students got off the bus one day, I called each by name and wished them a good afternoon. I said good-bye to Sharkie, because she is fond of an aquarium shirt with a shark on it. Then there was Hollywood, because I didn't know her name and she was wearing sunglasses one day. And so on.

I was unaware that a young lady behind me was listening as I commented to each person as they left the bus. When I pulled up to her house and called her by her actual name, she said, "Why don't I have a nickname?"

It was a reasonable question.

I thought about her personality, not a tomboy but not girly-girly, either. Well, maybe attire, some days a cute girl outfit, others days shorts, T-shirt, and tennis shoes. This could prove difficult. But before I had a chance to render my verdict, she said, "I want to be called 'Tex.'"

So, Tex it is.

You never really know what lies deep in the heart of a person. It may be a dusty old cowboy.

Tools of the Trade

Phrases that all bus driver need to familiarize themselves with:

Please be seated. Thank you.

Stop licking the windows. They've already been cleaned today.

Stop licking the seat. It will cause a blister on your tongue.

Stop licking the person next to you. People don't taste that good.

No, you cannot get off at the gas station and get a Coke. Unless you're buying for everyone.

Put the handcuffs up. No, I'm not sure why your parents would have them.

Leave the cactus up here by me. It might get damaged by the other kids.

No, I cannot close my eyes for you to do a magic trick. Can you make yourself disappear?

Stop swinging your underwear over your head and put them up. Yes, I'm glad they're clean.

Yes, I know his grandfather was only wearing boxer shorts with 'Sugar Baby' written on them. Wasn't it nice for him to walk him to the bus?

Those dogs are only wrestling. They must be good friends.

Yes, I know the bus is hot, darling. But you need to put your shirt back on.

Icing on the Cake

The bus made several slow turns down into the river bottom. During the night it had rained, washing everything clean. Now the rising sun was glistening off the gold of the hickory trees, the reds of the maples, and the yellows and browns of the oaks.

Turning, I followed the edge of the river. Off to the right, deer were browsing in a cornfield that had been harvested. Squirrels scampered across the road as they collected the bountiful harvest.

God, through nature, had painted an autumn picture that not even the most talented artist could attempt. Ignoring the racket behind me I thought, "How could this morning be any better?"

As if in answer to my thoughts, a young lady handed me a rectangular piece of paper that had writing on it. She said it was a 99,000-dollar bill and she wanted me to have it.

Icing on the cake. Retirement just moved a little closer.

The Lookout

A warning cry pierced the usual din of the bus—"Take cover!"

I looked in the mirror and there was the watchman, or in this case the watchwoman. A kindergartener with her hair in long pigtails was standing in the seat. With a look of urgency, she shouted again, "Take cover!"

I and many riders scanned the horizon expecting the onslaught of an aerial bombardment, but all seemed to be clear.

I glanced back just in time to see pigtails sail across the aisle in a rather surprising leap. She popped up from behind the seat. I'm thinking, this can't be some type of flashback; she's a kindergartener and doesn't have enough years to flash back on.

As she peered over the back of the seat there was one last cry of warning, "Everybody take cover!" Then she disappeared behind the seat.

I'm now thinking it's trauma due to an overzealous teacher during a tornado drill.

Facing Mortality

At one time or another, we have all thought of the end, the final day, our last breath. For most, death comes at an unknown hour but for some it could come at a given period of time.

We sometimes ask ourselves what would I do if I knew the time? This was the question that was posed one day by one young student to another.

The first said, "What would you do if you were on Hawaii and you knew it was going to blow up in thirty-six hours?" The other student answered, "Leave Hawaii."

I was in complete agreement. However, this was not the thought provoking response that was desired, so he tried again. "What would you do if you knew the whole world would blow up in thirty-six hours?"

This was more to the point and took a little more time in thought, though not as much as you might expect. Student No. 2's eyebrows went down; you could tell he was pondering the end, the certain mortality of man.

After a surprisingly short time for such a weighty question, he responded with the certainty of a man with a plan that would surely give him peace of mind as he prepared to meet his maker.

"Well," he said, "I guess I would go to my room and eat some Beanee Weenees." He noticed the blank looks on the faces around him and added, "They're really pretty good."

So the next time someone comes up to you and says,

"You look like you could use a can of Beanee Weenees," you might want to make sure things are in order.

Miles to Go and a Promise to Keep

The first thing he said to me after we exchanged the usual pleasantries was, "Mr. Brandon, I'm hungry."

It wasn't an unusual statement, especially from him. So I reassured him that we would soon be at school and he could get some breakfast.

"No," he protested, "I'm really hungry. Could we stop at the Waffle House?"

I have to admit the idea of some covered, smothered, and chunked hash browns was appealing. But before I could give the negative response that should have been obvious, he pleaded again, "Come on, Mr. Brandon. Let's stop at the Waffle House."

Knowing the bond of trust that is between driver and student, I proceeded cautiously, "I tell you what we'll do. If we pass a Waffle House on our route today, I will pull in and let you order anything you want."

A satisfied smile spread across his face and all was right in the world. So, as the big yellow limo rumbled on down the road on a route that we had traveled so many times that every house, tree, trash can, and dog was familiar to both of us, he sat back in complete contentment, mumbling to himself what all he was going to order if we passed a Waffle House.

Mmmmmm.

Thanks, UPS

As we approached Hot Pickle Boy's house, he asked if I would slow down so he could look for something. In the afternoons, he does not get off the bus at his house. He goes to his grandmother's house, just a few doors down, until his mother gets home.

But he wanted me to slow down so he could look on the porch. He was expecting a delivery from UPS. He said he had saved up some money and had ordered something and wanted to see if it had arrived.

Now to say that Hot Pickle Boy is country and has unusual tastes is like saying that dogs crave attention and cats only look at you with disgust. It's just understood.

He was not forthcoming with what he had ordered but assured me that when it came in, he would let me see it.

Several days went by of slowing in front of his house and looking, to no avail. After about a week he boarded the bus one morning and said the package had arrived and he had brought it for me to look at. But in typical kid fashion I had to guess what it was, with the hint, starts with a "G" ends with an "S."

I ran through my mental Hot Pickle Boy archives. Hunting or fishing gear was the most likely items, but my attempts to guess were fruitless, so he decided to move on to the unveiling.

He unzipped his book bag and pulled out an Israeli military gas mask. He showed me how it fit and how the filter canister was attached to the front. He then modeled it for me, then turned and walked down the aisle, still wearing the gas mask, took his seat.

I would have liked to have had a clever quote or a deep philosophical thought at this time, but I just didn't know what to say about looking in the rearview mirror at a student wearing a rubber, military gas mask while riding my bus.

Dreams Die Hard

It was almost the first of February, but one of those days that could fool you into believing that spring was just around the corner.

It was warm enough outside that I opened the driver's window to let air circulate to keep the bus from getting stuffy from all those little warm bodies. Students were excitedly talking about how they were going to play outside when they got home.

Then, in all the excitement, there was a sound that was out of place. It started low but began to grow in volume. I looked in the rearview mirror for the source of the sound of someone crying.

Now crying on a school bus is not an unusual occurrence. It quite often is coming from the driver, but that's another story. Yet this was not just crying. It was on the verge of what I would term as weeping. I located the source and there she sat with tears rolling down her little round face. One look at her and you couldn't help but think, "Whoever made this baby cry is in serious trouble."

The boy sitting next to her was the obvious choice. This would not be the first little girl he made cry.

I did what any man with a daughter and a granddaughter would do. I gave the suspect the evil eye and at the same time said, "Come here, baby, and tell Mr. Brandon what's wrong."

There was a pause while I waited for the sobbing to come under control so I could understand what she was saying. During this pause, all I could think about was how much trouble that boy was going to be in.

Finally catching her breath, she was able to tell me

the heart-wrenching details: "Mr. Brandon, I wanted a spaceship for Christmas and I didn't get one."

She then turned the tears back on.

I would have gladly given her a spaceship if I had one, but no luck. Trying to ease her pain, I explained that I had not received a spaceship for Christmas, either. Then we took a quick survey of the four front seats. No one had gotten a spaceship for Christmas. This did not dry up the flow of tears, but they did ebb somewhat.

When dreams die, solace is often difficult to find.

Invitation

Mr. Mucus was excitedly telling about a big event coming up, a special evening with his Boy Scout troop called the Blue and Gold dinner. He described it as a dinner that the family is invited to so the young men who have been in scouts that year can be honored.

He was quite excited.

He paused and then said, "Mr. Brandon, I would like for you to come. I mean, you are a big part of my life." In my mind, I thought, yes, Kindergarten, First Grade, First Grade again (because, as he puts it, he was not quite ready to move on), and now we were nearing the end of Second Grade.

One year alone, I had to clean up the bus more than twenty times from him getting sick. He had shared his imagination with me, from him being a secret agent to conversations he had with his wife over the phone. He had shown me his awesome dance moves and given advice on how to drive the bus route.

Yes, he had been a big part of my life also. He then put his hand on my shoulder and said, "I mean, I love you like a brother, man."

Some things can make you laugh and smile at the same time. *Pleasant words are as an honeycomb, sweet to the soul, and health to the bones* (Proverbs 16:24).